EASY SBA

1 Step-by-step guide to apply for a small business loan

Claire Wood

To my husband for his constant support.

EASY SBA

1 Step-by-step guide to apply for a small business loan

CONTENTS

Introduction

Congratulations reader! You made the first step towards obtaining an SBA (U.S. Small Business Administration) small business loan by buying this book. Because you are (or want to become) a business owner, you want funds to grow or start your business and your time is precious. You need something quick and easy to read, a simple guide that gets to the point, with the best advice and tips. **After reading this book, you will be amazed at how easy it will be to get approved for the most famous SBA loan for small businesses.**

A little bit about me: I have been working in the finance, banking and lending industry for many years. My experience includes working as a lender representing banks, and as a loan packager working with clients like yourself who are seeking loans. I have held underwriting positions in banks and with a FinTech startup packaging SBA loans for banks. I have helped hundreds of small business owners like you with their applications.

In my work with small business owners, it became clear to me that for many applicants the SBA loan was their first business loan and so was unfamiliar to them. They often had a hard time understanding eligibility standards and following the steps to complete their applications. New business owners know their core business but often struggle to understand some of the basic concepts around a bank loan. This is perfectly understandable and normal as it's all new.

The purpose of this book is to give you step-by-step instructions to get your application in order quickly and to take the fear and stress out of the process. **Knowledge is power and this book will give you the power in the SBA application process.**

We review in this book the traditional SBA 7(a) loan program's benefits, how it can fit your needs, how to see if you can qualify for it and how to successfully apply for it. I will give you tips and knowledge that I learnt myself while being an SBA 7(a) loan underwriter. I will explain the most current and used underwriting guidelines and share anecdotes from applicants I worked with. Each lender has its own regulations which can differ from a State to another, so if you don't qualify with one you could still qualify with another. You must be excited to learn more so let's define what an SBA 7(a) loan is.

2

Part One

SBA 7(a) Loan

The 7(a) Loan is the SBA primary program for helping start-ups and existing small businesses for general business purposes. **Let's be clear, the SBA is not lending money itself to the businesses. It guarantees loans made by participating lending institutions.** These lenders are national and regional banks, credit unions, loans organization and other financing institutions that are approved by the Small Business Administration to lend funds to small businesses, under the SBA programs specifics conditions, to be guaranteed partially by the SBA in the event of borrower default. It reduces the lender's risk, as it is mitigated by the SBA guarantee, lending institutions are more willing to provide loans for businesses. **Therefore, the SBA helps businesses get a loan that they won't be able to get through a normal business lending process**.

SBA 7(a) loans have many advantages besides being business loans backed up by the government. They have the lowest interest rates available on the market, the lowest monthly payments, a long-term loan available (10 years), and low origination fees. The 7(a)-loan program can fund up to $5 million maximum per applicant. Surprisingly, the average loan amount in the last couple of years has been around $375,000.

Chapter One

The best working capital loan for small businesses

I. Lowest rates

The interest rate for a 7(a) loan can be negotiated between the applicant and the lender, but the SBA sets maximums to ensure lowest costs for small business owners. Good news for you!

7(a) loan Interest Rate = Base Rate + Allowable Spread

Base Rate: the lender can choose between 3 acceptable base rates. The most widely used benchmark for lending is the **Prime Rate** (which is the lowest rate of interests at which funds can be borrowed commercially to non-bank customers). Lenders can use a different benchmark than the Prime Rate, like the 1-month London Interbank Offered Rate plus a margin or SBA's optional PEG rate.

Allowable Spread: In addition to the base rate, the lender can set a margin, which is limited by the SBA depending on the maturity of the loan.

- If the loan has a maturity under 7 years, the spread (margin) can NOT be more than 2.25%.
- If the loan has a maturity over 7 years, the spread (margin) can NOT be more than 2.75%.

These base rates can go up or down based on the market conditions. The Prime Rate is governed by the Federal Reserve System (FED). Since September 2017 the United States Prime Rate remains at 4.25%. Most of the credit products are based on this benchmark, therefore don't be afraid of the word "variable", it can go down like it can go up. This would be the case for most of your other debts, except for fixed rate products. What is important to compare is the Annual Percentage Rate (APR). It is the amount of interest, including all fees associated to your loan like broker fees, closing costs, on your total loan amount, that you'll pay annually (averaged over the full term of the loan). This will help you compare the offers from different lenders. A lower APR indicates lower monthly payments.

If I lost you in this paragraph, not to worry. You can always ask the lender to specify his APR for the SBA loan offer and compare it with other offers you may have.

II. Longest term

This program's maturity can be between **5 to 10 years maximum** for general business purpose, like refinancing, equipment purchase, working capital and hiring. It is a fixed maturity. Generally, there will be higher interest rates for loans over 7 years term.

Imagine how convenient this can be for your business, you have 10 years to repay the loan, where most alternative lenders will ask full pay back in less than a year or two. You avoid the stress of diverting funds to loan repayment and can manage the way you want to use the funds to grow your business and generate more revenues.

III. Lowest monthly payments

Because of low interest rates and long-term maturity, **the monthly payments are the lowest available on the market!** This is GREAT NEWS for your business, as it will help avoid the classic "cash flow problem" that many business owners can face with expensive loans at higher rates and shorter duration.

For the SBA loan the borrower usually has a monthly payment comprised of principal and interest. In most cases it is debited by ACH from the business's account to avoid any missed payment and insure payment in full every month.

IV.   No prepayment penalty and no balloon payment

The SBA does not allow a balloon payment for 7(a) loans, it must be fully amortized.

A balloon payment means that during the term of the loan you did not pay off the full borrowed amount. With the SBA loan, the full loan amount is amortized over the term and you pay the same monthly payments until the loan is paid off with no large final payment.

Some loans can include penalties if the loan is paid off earlier than its term. This is fortunately not the case in the SBA loan. The borrower can make prepayments on his 7(a) loan without paying penalties at any time.

V. Low origination fees

Origination fees can vary usually from 2% to 6% in total, charged either from one entity or several ones if they have all worked toward different steps of the loan process. Fees can go to a broker for a referral fee and/or a loan provider who underwrites and packages your loan documents. The lender will charge closing costs. If you work directly with the lender, it might be the cheapest option to avoid broker and loan provider fees. The loan provider will help you get your loan faster but you will need to work closely with him and provide a list of documents that we will see in Part 2 Chapter 3.

This book is intended to help you reduce origination fees. This book tells you how to package your loan yourself and avoid the cost of intermediaries between you and the lender. This book can also be used if you work with a loan provider or broker, helping you speed up the process by having documentation necessary.

VI.   No guarantee fee for loan amount up to $150,000

The SBA can guarantee:
- up to 85% of a loan up to $150,000
- up to 75% of a loan greater than $150,000.

The maximum SBA exposure is $3,750,000 (for loan of $5 millions).

The SBA assess a guarantee fee to guaranty the loan. The fee is based on the loan's maturity and the amount guaranteed (not on the total loan amount).

- **For loan amount up to $150,000 = NO SBA FEE!**
- For loan amount $150,001 to $700,000 = 3% of the guaranteed portion
- For loan amount $700,001 to $5,000,000 = 3.5% of the guaranteed portion + an additional 0.25% for any guaranteed portion > $1 million.

Examples of SBA guarantee fee:

- For loan amount $200,000 the guaranteed portion is 75% of $200,000 = $150,000. The SBA fee is 3% of that guaranteed portion so 3% of $150,000 = $4,500.

- For loan amount of $800,000 the guaranteed portion is 75% of $800,000 = $600,000. The SBA fee is 3.5% of that guaranteed portion so 3.5% of $600,000 = $21,000.

- For loan amount of $2,000,000 the guaranteed portion is 75% of $2,000,000 = $1,500,000. The SBA fee is 3.5% of that guaranteed portion plus 0.25% of the guaranteed portion over $1 million, which means 0.25% on $500,00. We have the first 3.5% of $1,500,000 = $52,500 plus an additional 0.25% of $500,000 = $1,250, therefore total SBA fee = $52,500+$1,250=$53,750.

Tip
If you are looking for a loan amount close to $150,000 it is worth it to not go over that amount if you don't have the need for more cash flow. That way you avoid paying thousands of dollars in the SBA guarantee fee.

SBA guarantee fee for loan amount >$150,000:
- $170,000 loan amount, the SBA fee is $3,825
- $200,000 loan amount, the SBA fee is $4,500
- $230,000 loan amount, the SBA fee is $5,175
- $260,000 loan amount the SBA fee is $5,850
- $300,000 loan amount, the SBA fee is $6,750
- $350,000 loan amount the SBA fee is $7,875

VII. Collateral

This SBA loan is collateralized. The lender will take any business or personal collateral as available to secure the 7(a) loan up to the loan amount. What this means is if the business owns only one computer then that's the collateral. If the business owns a commercial building or land, equipment, tools, vehicles, then they will all be included in the collateral assets list. They will have liens on them, putting the SBA lender in the best position available. They can be positioned after lien holders that are already in place for current debts.

The SBA expects 7(a) loans to be as fully secured as possible (exception: the SBA does not require the lender to take collateral for loans under $25,000). If a borrower has a strong application with many strengths but has insufficient collateral, the lack of value in collateral will not be an obstacle to the 7(a) loan. **The SBA cannot decline a loan based on insufficient collateral if all available assets have been offered and still do not equal the loan amount value. This is a major advantage especially for businesses with little assets that struggle getting business loan through regular lending process because of lack of collateral.**

There are no restrictions on what the lender can ask as collateral. If the business assets are insignificant, the lender can ask for personal assets of the principal owners to secure the loan.

Personal guarantees are required from all guarantors (owners of at least 20% of the business's equity or owner's spouse owning 5% or more of the business). Lenders can choose to require also the personal guarantees of owners with less than 20% in the business ownership. Personal guaranties are not an unusual feature for a business loan, most business loans are personally guaranteed.

VIII. Use of proceeds

The SBA 7(a) loan can be used for many business general purposes including:

- convert, expand or renovate buildings
- acquire and install fixed assets, equipment, machinery
- acquire inventory
- purchase supplies and raw materials
- leasehold improvements
- working capital
- refinance eligible business outstanding debts
- hiring
- marketing and advertising

Real estate acquisition building or land, finance a start-up and purchase a business can be financed by a 7(a) loan but in terms of underwriting it requires a longer process and more documentation. These are not discussed in this book.

Refinancing outstanding business debts is possible if they are eligible. The debts must be in the business name and have been used only for business purposes. If the debt being refinanced by the SBA was also a refinanced debt, the first debt must also be eligible (in the business name and used only for business purpose).

Tip
Make sure you keep the history of your business debts (promissory note, statements, payment history). If a personal debt was refinanced by a business debt, that business debt is not eligible to be refinanced by the SBA, because at the origin it was a personal loan.

Attention:

- You can NOT use the funds to refinance personal debts, it should be in the business name and the funds must have been use for business purposes.
- You can NOT use the funds to pay taxes, whether business or personal taxes, this is strictly prohibited.
- You can NOT use the funds for construction, some lenders will allow to use no more than $10,000 unless the lender specifically allow a greater amount for construction, be sure to discuss this use with the lender.
- You can NOT use the funds for a change of ownership of the business that does not benefit the company.
- You can NOT use the funds to reimburse an owner that injected equity or capital in the company to help the business continue while waiting for the SBA loan.
- You can NOT use the funds for any purpose that is not considered a business purpose.

There are alternative lenders that can help you with these SBA prohibited uses of proceeds.

Chapter Two

Eligibility

There are only a few conditions to be an eligible business for the 7(a) loan.

The business must be eligible, the owner(s) must qualify for the loan as the guarantor(s) for their own company's debt and the use of the funds must be eligible as defined by the SBA.

We will review in this section these eligibility requirements, as well as the considerations regarding specific situations. We will list industries prohibited from 7(a) loan application and cases when a company or an owner can become ineligible to apply.

I. Eligible business: size and nature of the business

To be eligible for an SBA 7(a) loan, the small business applicant must be an operating business, organized for profit, located in the United States, be "small" as defined by SBA and demonstrate a need for credit to grow the business. The owner must have reasonable equity invested in the business. It must have used alternative financial resources, including personal assets, before asking for financial assistance from the SBA. It can be a start-up business; these applicants are less often granted a 7(a) loan as the risks are higher for the lender than a business that has two years of history to show.

The SBA has three size standards to be considered an eligible "small" business:

- **Maximum of 500 employees** for most manufacturing and mining industries.
- **Maximum $7.5 million in average annual receipts** for many non-manufacturing industries.
- The business **cannot have a tangible net worth exceeding $15 million and an average net income greater than $5 million over the past two years**.

There are exceptions that you can find online on the Table of Small Business Size Standards on www.sba.gov, searching by your NAICS code (North American Industry Classification System).

Some businesses and individuals can be eligible according to special considerations:

> **Franchises:**

They are eligible except when the franchisor retains some control over certain operations. The franchisee must have the right to benefit directly from efforts commensurate with ownership. Before January 2017, to be eligible they would have to be listed on the "SBA Franchise Registry" that shows approved franchises.

Since January 2017 the SBA revised its regulations governing affiliations and put in place a unique form, not only for franchises, but for other businesses not defined themselves as franchises. This form is an addendum to the existing agreement between franchisor and franchisee, the form can be adapted a bit, see the instructions form in the appendix of this book, look the form 2462 and its instructions). Therefore, any business affiliated with an agent agreement, license agreement, or relationship agreement, are now defined as "franchise" in regard to the SBA loan eligibility if they meet the definition set by the Federal Trade Commission.

The most common example of business now considered "franchise" is the Insurance Agent. Even if he is independent, he has an agent agreement between him and the agency from which he sell the insurance policies and products. An insurance agency applying for an SBA 7(a) loan will need to get this franchise SBA form 2462 (attached in the appendix of this book) signed by its agency representative and himself. If they can't get it signed, the insurance agent is unfortunately ineligible for the SBA loan.

Tip
If you are in this situation, either an insurance agent or unsure about your agreement, don't lose time packaging your loan documents before you get form 2462 signed with your "franchisor", "distributor", "Agency" or "licensor". Or at least talk about this form to the franchisor to get their consent they will sign it, should you get the SBA loan.

> **Farms and agricultural businesses**

Farms and agricultural businesses are required to have first approached the Farm Service Agency before trying to get a loan from the SBA.

> **Medical facilities and Convalescent and nursing homes**

They are eligible if they are licensed by the appropriate government agency and the services rendered go beyond room and board.

Instead of naming all the industries that are eligible per their activity for a 7(a) loan, the SBA listed industries that are NOT eligible by nature, check the list below to verify if your business is not part of it. If you have doubt, ask your SBA lender, it will let you know right away.

Businesses that are NOT eligible per SBA guidelines[1]:

- Non-profit businesses (for profit subsidiaries are eligible)
- Financial businesses primarily engaged in the business of lending, such as banks, finance companies, and factors;
- Passive businesses owned by developers and landlords that do not actively use or occupy the assets acquired or improved with the loan proceeds (except Eligible Passive Companies);
- Life insurance companies;
- Businesses located in a foreign country (businesses in the U.S. owned by aliens may qualify)
- Pyramid sales distribution plans;
- Businesses deriving more than one-third of gross annual revenue from legal gambling activities;
- Businesses engaged in any illegal activity;
- Private clubs and businesses which limit the number of memberships for reasons other than capacity;
- Government-owned entities (except for businesses owned or controlled by a Native American tribe);
- Businesses principally engaged in teaching, instructing, counseling or indoctrinating religion or religious beliefs, whether in a religious or secular setting;
- Consumer and marketing cooperatives (producer cooperatives are eligible);
- Loan packagers earning more than one third of their gross annual revenue from packaging SBA loans;
- Businesses with an Associate who is incarcerated, on probation, on parole, or has been indicted for a felony or a crime of moral turpitude;
- Businesses in which the lender or any of its Associates owns an equity interest;
- Businesses which present live performances of a prurient sexual nature; or derive directly or indirectly more than 5% of their gross revenue through the sale of products or services, or the presentation of any depictions or displays, of a prurient sexual nature;

---

[1] Source: list quoted from the SBA Standard Operating Procedures 50 10 5(I) effective since 01/01/2017.

- A business or applicant involved in a business which defaulted on a Federal loan or federally assisted financing resulting in a loss to the government. A compromise agreement shall also be considered a loss;
- Businesses primarily engaged in political or lobbying activities;
- Speculative businesses (such as oil wildcatting).

I have not seen many ineligible businesses, the few recurring ones that were not eligible were usually real estate owners renting their properties for profit (business revenues being only rent, and no property management involved), ATM businesses and religious institutions.

It is possible to apply to an SBA 7(a) loan as a start-up business. Chances of getting funded are low, due to the risk for the lender, the lack of financial history, possible lack of experience and low collateral to pledge. **In this book we will focus on businesses with at least 2 years of history.**

II. Eligible guarantors

Both the business and the guarantor(s) must be eligible. This is a very important fact. Even a profitable business must have an eligible guarantor

The owner of a business is considered guarantor if he/she owns at least 20% of the business. A business can have multiple guarantors. Each guarantor must be eligible according to the SBA guidelines. In the case of a business owned by a married couple, if one spouse owns less than 20% but at least 5% of the business, that spouse will be a guarantor. The guarantor is the person who will be responsible to repay the debt should the borrower (the business entity) fails to make its payments.

Each guarantor must:

A. Be a United States Citizen or a Lawful Permanent Resident of the United States, at least 21 years old.

If you are a U.S. citizen, you can provide the lender your driver license, State ID or your passport. If you are not a U.S. citizen but you have a Legal Permanent Resident status (you have the "green card"), you are eligible, you will provide copy of your passport and of your Green Card, complete a form G-845 (see appendix of this book). Local SBA districts can verify status for cases when you are legally living and working in the United States but have not yet received a green card. This status is case by case. The lender and the SBA put these conditions to avoid non- U.S. citizen resident to default on their loan and leave the country, leaving the debt unpaid. When exception is made to grant an SBA loan for a legal resident without a green card, the lender is required to have the loan value 100% collateralized with business and/or personal assets of same or higher value. It can take the form of a financial investment or a real estate secured for the lender.

B. Have a "good character"

The SBA and the lender require the owner and its business partners to meet the definition of "good character" to be eligible for the loan. The good character criteria is based on the personal history, integrity and any past criminal record.

It is difficult to measure the "good character" of a person. While there is no "checklist" for it, the lender will pay attention during conversations to your attitude, personality and tone. They will sense if they can trust your commitment to repay the loan, they examine your reasons for the loan. If they find something "iffy" in your story, they will probably decline your application.

The lender has experience with borrowers and can detect when something is off. It is part of their due diligence to scrutinize every aspect of the business and its owner(s).

Tip
Be there AND be square! Be fully invested in your application with the underwriter, be honest and don't play hide and seek when he asks for more information. Relax, keep it nice and polite, he is here to help you get a loan. Be forthcoming and ask as many questions as you need, it's your business and your loan application, you want to make it right so don't be shy to ask when things get confusing. You will be just fine!

Anecdote: I have seen applicants ruin their application because they couldn't be trusted. I remember an applicant telling me one story one day and a different one the following day. The use of proceeds was not clear, he lied about insurance coverage and provided fake certificates. We gave him time for his credit score to recover from former inquiries so he could qualify, but he kept applying for other debt and took more debt during his application that he failed to disclose. Another applicant hid that his business was under a lawsuit, and lied about the real use of proceeds of the loan.

Good character also relies on the applicant's criminal history, if any. Each principal[2], senior staff[3] or any other individual guarantor on the loan, who has any criminal record must complete form 912. They must disclose if they have been arrested in the last six months and why. Do not worry, you will not be disqualified for a minor motor vehicle violation, or if the crime has been discharged.

Anecdote: I have seen many applicants pass the 912 process and get their loan. Some had discharged offenses linked with use of drugs in the past, some had DUI when they were in their 20's. Offenses involving gun and violence can be an issue. Because of the long timeline, applicants in need of funds with 912 issues are often encouraged to pursue another lending route.

The 912 process

Depending on the degree of the offense (felony or misdemeanor), it might take few weeks or even few months for the lender to obtain clearance from the SBA. The applicant submits the form 912 and usually 2 or 3 other documents. The SBA will verify the information provided and run a background check. Always be trustworthy in your answers.

a **912 from** (see book's appendix) Everyone concerned complete the first part with their personal ID information, and answer 3 questions:

⇒ <u>Question #7</u>

Are you presently subject to an indictment, criminal information, arraignment, or other means by which formal criminal charges are brought in any jurisdiction? Yes/No

NO = No issue.
YES = DISQUALIFICATION, the application is declined. Principals or senior staff on probation or parole, or current indicted or incarcerated, are not eligible for the SBA loan. They can't run a business and pay back the loan while they are in jail or risk going to prison.

---

[2] A principal of a business is a general term that includes the following roles: sole proprietor, general partner, director, managing member, officer, owner with at least 20% of the business shares.

[3] A person is considered senior staff when he/she holds a day-to-day management position. The senior staff does not guaranty personally the loan, usually only his/her ID and basic ID information is required, no financial documents require, but good character is mandatory.

⇒   Question #8

Have you been arrested in the past six months for any criminal offense? Yes/No

NO = No issue.
YES = It is not an auto decline, it needs further information about the offense. See next question.

⇒   Question #9

For any criminal offense – other than a minor vehicle violation – have you ever: 1) been convicted; 2) plead guilty; 3) plead nolo contendere; 4) been placed on pretrial diversion; or 5) been placed on any form of parole or probation (including probation before judgment).

NO = No issue.
YES = If you had 1 misdemeanor not prosecuted, the process can be cleared quickly without the SBA. If you had more than 3 misdemeanors prosecuted, or more than 1 misdemeanor for the last 10 years, or any felony, the SBA clearance is mandatory to continue and background check + fingerprints will be required.

If an applicant answered yes to question 8 or/and 9, he is usually required by the lender to provide all or some of the following documents as well:

b   **Copy of all Court documents:** even if the case was settled.

c   **Written explanation:** write a letter with your full name for every offense, that explains what happened, when and where it took place, if it was a felony or misdemeanor, if a fine was paid.

d   **Fingerprint card:** go to myfbireport.com to search by ZIP code the closest agency location for you to go to get your fingerprints taken.

When all the documents are submitted to the lender, he will provide them to the SBA to get clearance as soon as possible. At this point the lender is not in control of the turnover, the process can take few weeks only or few months depending on the criminal records.

Tip
If you have a criminal record, do not hide it, make sure to get the 912 process started right away with your lender, as soon as other key eligibility factors have been checked. If you are in a hurry to get funds you might discuss with your lender the possibility of using alternative lending in the meantime. If the 912 process comes back clear and all other

> eligibility requirements are fulfilled a temporary bridge loan can be refinanced into the new SBA 7(a) loan.

C. Have good credit history

Credit management and your credit score will be assessed during an SBA loan application. **Lenders require different minimum credit scores; each guarantor must reach the minimum**. The underwriter will scrutinize in detail the full credit report. The report provides the history of all debts acquired since your first credit product, like a credit card or student loan. It shows your payment history, any charge offs, collections, the most recent minimum monthly payments, credit inquiries, type of credit, and the outstanding balance due for each debt.

Lenders will be attentive to the total revolving balance amount. A revolving balance is the portion of the credit card balance that is unpaid at the end of the billing cycle. An applicant with high revolving balance represents a higher risk and triggers the following questions: why such a high amount? What are the funds used for?

Tip
An applicant should reduce his credit cards balance as much as possible. This will improve your credit score. If you still have a high revolving balance outstanding (high can be considered above $35,000 in credit cards), write an explanation. This will help the underwriter understand the situation. Explain in your own words what happened that led to that balance and provide further explanation on how you plan to pay it down. Remember, the SBA loan can NOT be used to pay down your personal credit cards. If you injected money in your business with your personal credit cards, that is acceptable. If the credit cards were used for other personal family events, home remodeling or purchase a car, show the lender the plan to lower the balance in the coming months.

If the individual has a high revolving balance the day his credit report was pulled, but it was subsequently paid off, you can show proof to your lender. The judgement on the revolving balance can also be mitigated if the individual has high income and the balance fits his "lifestyle". If the balance is paid down in full every month, this won't be an issue.

The minimum credit score required is reviewed in further detail in Part 2 of this book.

D. Be in good standing with the IRS

The guarantor must have filed his taxes every year and if there is an outstanding balance owed to the IRS, it MUST be paid in full or be part of an installment agreement. **The guarantor must not have any pending tax lien**. This is very important and I want to emphasize this as a high priority before you apply for an SBA loan considering the delay it can take to clear it off (4 to 8 weeks!).

Tip
If you owe the IRS less than $50,000 for your personal taxes, you can visit the IRS website to enter into an installment agreement within 5 minutes. Make your first payment and print out the receipt as well as the confirmation page.
If you owe the IRS $50,000 or more for your personal taxes, the installment agreement can't be set up online. You will need to either call the IRS or visit your local IRS center. It might be faster for you to set this up during a face to face appointment with an agent in a local IRS center, as you can get a copy of your repayment plan right away. If you are setting it up by phone the process might take from 4 to 8 weeks.
If your business owes the IRS you can apply for an installment agreement online if the balance owed is less than $25,000. If the business owes more, you will need to call the IRS or visit a local IRS center to set up a repayment plan.

Anecdotes: Most of borrowers who owe the IRS know it and half of the time don't set up an installment agreement. I have seen the best-case scenario and the worst. Best: the applicant was in a hurry to get it done and could resolve the issue online and get the documents right away. Worst: the applicant let the situation "rot" and thought the underwriter could do it in his place (false). It was a nightmare to deal with, while it would have run so smoothly if the borrower had the repayment plan in place before applying.

If you have not filed one or more years of your taxes, whether business or personal returns, you must absolutely file them before applying for the SBA loan. Lenders will need proof of filing for late filing. They will order tax transcripts to see the records of account for you and your business (if you file separately), to check that the transcripts match the tax returns you provided. The lender will verify in detail if the numbers are the same, the transcripts will indicate the amount owed to IRS if any, it will indicate if an installment agreement is set up and paid in due time. If the tax transcripts of one year comes back empty, it means that this year was not filed. You may have the option to e-file, check this with your accountant or CPA. Otherwise get these tax returns completed the soonest for the years missing and schedule an appointment with your local IRS center to file them. Make sure you bring 2 copy sets for each year not filed, so one set stays with the IRS agent and the other set needs to be stamped with the official IRS stamp "FILED ON MM/DD/YYYY" that copy is for the lender as proof of filing (keep a copy of course for your records).

Tip
You can get your own tax transcripts online for free within few minutes. Go on www.irs.gov/individuals/get-transcript , click on "Get Transcript Online" and follow the instructions. It is great source of information for your records. You can ask for the last four years. You could also call IRS and have them mailed to you.

Tax lien

If an individual or a business owes more than $10,000 in unpaid taxes, the IRS has the right to file a lien against that taxpayer. **An outstanding IRS lien is an auto decline for your application**. The lien from the IRS must be released, whether it is filed on the County level and/or on the Federal level. You can contact your Secretary of State and do an UCC[4] search for any outstanding lien against you or your business. This will provide you the tax lien number and amount owed. Some States allow UCC searches to be done online for free.

Tip
I suggest you do your own UCC search. Go online and type the words in the search bar "UCC business" and the State the business is located. Then search your business name or search by business owner name, to find out if you have any lien. If there are liens from debts already paid off you can "clean them up" to remove old and expired liens.

---

[4] UCC= Uniform Commercial Code are a set of laws, adopted fully or partially by States in the USA, to uniform business and commercial transactions. We use "UCC search" to define the search for a listing of debts linked to a business name in a certain State. "UCC lien" means a lien against a business as shown on the UCC search, either as active or inactive.

E. Not have defaulted on government backed up loan

An applicant who defaulted on a government backed up loan, no matter how long ago, is automatically disqualified for an SBA loan. It could be a federally backed student loan, a government backed mortgage (FHA mortgages = Federal Housing Administration), or any type of SBA loan, a default on these loans is on the applicant's records forever. Unfortunately, the government does not give a second chance if there is a history of a prior default on a government backed up loan, even if it was discharged in a bankruptcy.

When an applicant fails to pay his taxes, it is also considered a loss to the government and that can be reported, like a default as well. Both defaults to pay create losses to the government which explains why the SBA is reluctant to guarantee a new loan to that individual or business entity.

If you fail to disclose a prior default on these types of loans at the early stage of your application, you will be simply wasting your time, as the lender will find out eventually and decline the application. The lender needs to pull your business SBA score, commonly named ETRAN score. That score needs to pass the minimum score of 145.

An outstanding FHA mortgage or an SBA loan, or government guaranteed student loan, are allowed, if they are current (no late payments).

Anecdote: I have worked with applicants that deliberately hid their past SBA default until we discovered it when pulling the ETRAN score. Some applicants thought because the default happened a long time ago there would be no record of it. The record stay forever. Then some applicants honestly didn't know that they had defaulted on an SBA loan. **If you have any doubt check with the underwriter who can pull the ETRAN score early in the process.**

III. Eligible use of the funds: have a plan to grow your business

The SBA lender will expect that before a business applies for a 7(a) loan, its owner has himself invested his own funds or made reasonable efforts to find other sources of funds including family, friends, personal assets and alternative financing options. Ask yourself: "Why would the SBA back my business if I don't even risk a penny?" If the applicant believes in his company, naturally he will finance it if possible. It makes sense that sometimes even a profitable business will require more investment than the owner can afford on his own. **Hello there! SBA is happy to help!**

The SBA and the lender will check the eligibility of the use of proceeds. The 7(a) program can be used for general business purposes with a few restrictions. We listed earlier in this book what is allowed.

The SBA website gives the following list of basic uses of proceeds allowed, all lenders do not necessarily offer them in their 7(a) loan program. Some might choose for example to not allow funding for real estate purchase, construction or renovation, because it requires more resources and knowledge to underwrite these specific purposes.

Basic uses for 7(a) loan proceeds[5] include:

- To provide long-term working capital to pay operational expenses, accounts payable and/or to purchase inventory
- Short-term working capital needs, including seasonal financing, contract performance, construction financing and exporting
- Revolving funds based on the value of existing inventory and receivables, under special conditions
- To purchase equipment, machinery, furniture, fixtures, supplies or materials
- To purchase real estate, including land and building
- To construct a new building or renovate an existing building
- To establish a new business or assist in the acquisition, operation or expansion of an existing business
- To refinance existing business debt, under certain conditions

It is important you have a plan in mind for the use of the funds. The lender does not need necessarily a written business plan; in fact, some will be satisfied with a simple letter detailing how you plan to use the loan proceeds. You need to give more details than just "I need working capital funds to grow my business". This is the fun part. **The more you speak about your plan the better, it shows you believe in it and you are motivated to get your business to the next level**.

Tip
You can prepare in advance a page where you explain the business' trends for the last three years, then add a paragraph at the end detailing how you plan to use the funds

---

[5] Per the SBA website https://www.sba.gov/loans-grants/see-what-sba-offers/sba-loan-programs/general-small-business-loans-7a/use-7a-loan-proceeds

to help your business grow. **I made a template in the appendix of this book to help you write the business' trends, you can add a paragraph, following that page, about the use of proceeds**. Look at your business tax returns and your most recent profit and loss statement.

Ask yourself for each of the last three years and the interim period: "Why did my revenue decline or increase that year? Or how did it constantly grow? Why did my expenses go down or up? Why was the profit higher or less than the year before?" Think about why this happened and what decisions, actions, strategies, events, may have caused this. For example: you changed product line, suppliers, improved marketing, hired more staff, acquired new clients, purchased expensive equipment, had a medical leave, experienced bad weather conditions or seasonality impacts.

Then add a paragraph explaining in your own words how the money is going to be used. If you hire people, tell which roles, how many individuals. If you purchase equipment, detail why you need it and what it does for the product or service delivered. If you need more inventory, show the growing demand from your customers' base. If you are planning to do marketing, tell which media will be used or which marketing company will revamp your website for example. It is your own story here, your opportunity to show the lender your business growth objectives and how you plan to reach them. **Be confident, honest and keep explanations simple**. They are not expecting a novel, just a page or two would be quite enough!

If you refinance business debt, besides being an eligible debt, it needs to be for better terms. If the debt has reasonable terms and the SBA loan won't make a significant difference or even end up being more expensive, then that debt can't be eligible for refinancing. If credit card debt will be refinanced, the borrower must also certify that the credit card debt being refinanced was incurred exclusively for business purposes.

For each debt to refinance, be prepared to answer the following questions to the lender:

- How will the new loan benefit the financial condition of your business?
- Why was the debt incurred in the first place? What was the original use of proceeds?

You don't need to provide numbers or any complicated analysis, just compare current debt service to SBA debt service and the immediate advantage it can provide to your cash. Explain how the money you will save on lower payments will help you, for example to pay for more inventory or help with hiring needs.

Part Two

Package your loan application

Obtaining any business loan isn't always easy and yet it is the most immediate source of funding for most small businesses. Before you speak to your local SBA lender, you should be prepared to understand factors the bank will use to evaluate your application and have your loan package ready so the process will be seamless and fast. Being eligible per SBA guidelines is one thing, being eligible per lender's guidelines is another. The lender has a specialized credit team that will determine if you qualify under their credit standards as well.

Each deal is unique and while an underwriting for one loan can be different from another, in this book we use the most common practices and underwriting rules. **I helped hundreds of applicants package their application and underwrote hundreds of SBA 7(a) loans. Based on that experience and lenders I worked with from different States, I have identified the common pieces of their loan process that will help you get a document package ready.**

I am going to guide you so you can be on top of your loan application!

Chapter One

Check your credit report

We will review how to read and understand your full credit report. First let's talk about credit scores, then the account information analysis and end with the public records analysis.

I. The scores:

Your credit scores are important to determine if you qualify for this SBA loan. There are two scores we look at: your FICO score and your Liquid score.

The FICO Score is your personal credit score, the one used when you apply for credit cards, mortgage, personal loans, auto loans... **Typically lenders will need your FICO score to be at least 600**. Some lenders will ask that it reaches minimum 650-660, or even 700. Do not give up if you don't qualify with one lender, there are plenty of SBA lenders and each one sets their own minimum credit score.

The Liquid Score is your business credit score. Yes, your business is scored too! It will depend on many factors like your personal credit, if your business pays in full and in time its dues to suppliers, third parties (bills), lenders (business loans, business credit cards). There are ways online to check this business score as well as your personal score in the same time without hurting them. **Lenders will need your Liquid score usually to be higher than 140.**

Tip
Before you apply for a loan in general, set yourself up for success by paying down your credit cards balance and then allow about a week to see the credit score increase. **Make sure to not make any inquiry for 3 months before applying if possible, 99% of the time when you do credit shopping they will hard pull your score and it hurts your score each time, so do not play that game before applying for an SBA loan.** The advantage is that you can have time before they hard pull the score at the final stage of approval, to get an eligible number if you were close.

II. Credit accounts information

A. Accounts and inquiries analysis

The lenders will see how many closed and open accounts you have. If there are many accounts opened recently, it might look like a desperate need for credit which is not a good sign. **Things happen, my advice is if you have a good explanation, it is all negotiable with the lender**.

They can see the past few years' credit inquiries, by date and by lender's name. They can see if it matches any opened account on your report. If not, they will ask you for the 3 most recent months, what were the inquiries about and if you might end up opening an account while applying in the same time for the SBA loan. It is recommended to be fully honest. **To give you a better chance of approval, it is best you give up any other credit application pending, as the SBA route is by far the best choice for the reasons described before.**

Each account will show its current balance, the remaining term if any, the maximum credit limit if it is a revolving debt and the last minimum monthly payment due. The lender will pay attention to the percentage of revolving limit you are using. Being close to your maximum limit is not recommended, the lender will see it as an issue and doubt your ability to repay.

Cheer up, having high revolving balance is not a dead end for your application, if it can be explained and there are solutions to solve it.

B. Recent late payment analysis

The lenders will scrutinize your payment history over the last one to two years. Some will simply ask you an explanation of what happened that led to a late payment on a credit card, auto loan, mortgage or student loan or any other debt showing on your credit report. Again, there might be a good explanation, and if it was an "accident", you will be fine. But if you have repetitive late payments, it is not helpful to your application. Others might decline your application if a 30-day late payment happened in the last 90 days, if a 60-day late payment happened in the last six months or if a 90-day late payment occurred in the last 365 days.

Tip
To avoid late payment, it is recommended to set up auto-payments, it will avoid the

bad surprise of missing a payment and hurting your credit score as well. It will also give you piece of mind. Call the number on the back of your credit card to find out more.

III.Public Records Analysis

Bankruptcy: You can relax, you can apply for an SBA loan with a past bankruptcy, usually lenders will check that it has been discharged or dismissed at least more than 3 years ago, that time can vary. **If you have an open or recently discharged bankruptcy you won't qualify for an SBA loan**. Most lenders decline the application if the guarantor has more than one bankruptcy on its credit report.

Tip
Write a letter describing what happened that led to your bankruptcy and what steps you took to make sure it won't happen again. It is important for the lender to understand why you filed for bankruptcy. If you write the bankruptcy happened because of the "2008 financial crisis", that will not be a valid explanation. Of course, a world wild crisis does not help, but causes of a household bankruptcy are personal, not everyone went bankrupt after 2008, in fact some businesses have remained profitable. Don't be ashamed about it, bad things can happen to anybody and you shouldn't be hard on yourself, or shy to talk about it. Therefore, take time to really understand what happened that led to losing the ability to pay your debts, why there was a lost income or why the expenses increased higher than the income could support. You have learned from this dramatic event in your life, and you run now your own business, be proud of the person you are! **Not everyone has the courage to start their own business.**

Foreclosure: If you did not make your mortgage payments, the lender can repossess the home, which is called a foreclosure. If it happened to you at least 3 years ago some lenders would be fine with keeping you qualified, you will simply provide an explanation. It can be an auto decline for some banks, this is depending on lenders' credit policy.

Charge-offs: If you have not made payments on a debt for several months, the account might get closed and the creditor declares that the amount of the debt is unlikely to be collected. Lenders can either decline your application because of past charge-off accounts or be ok with it if the charge-off accounts are at least 12 months old.

Collections: If you have been delinquent or past due on an account, the creditor can transfer your debt to a third party (collection agency). The collection agency assumes the responsibility of collecting the debt for the original creditor. Collection accounts MUST be paid, otherwise you will be declined. Make sure you have no outstanding collection accounts, call the original creditor if necessary to resolve the issue and pay off the outstanding amount due.

Tip
Ask for a free credit report from a credit bureau to check if you have any collection accounts. You should know if you have any. Sometimes medical payments or phone bills can appear as collections if they are in a process of a dispute between you and the insurance company or phone company. Don't let these bills last too long, to avoid them becoming collection accounts. Especially if they are of small amounts, they can be resolved the same day.

Tax lien: is a lien imposed by law upon a property to secure the payment of taxes. If you failed to pay taxes owed on real property or on personal property, business taxes, or income taxes, any other taxes owed, the government can set up a claim against your property. You must be in good standing with the IRS to be eligible for an SBA loan. **You can't have open or outstanding tax liens**. As we mentioned in the first chapter of this book, you cannot use funds from an SBA loan to pay your taxes. If you have an accountant or CPA, confirm with him/her that you do not owe taxes. Some applicants may think because they have a payment plan set up to pay a tax lien, that the lien is released: I am afraid to inform you this is "fake news". The lien will be released once the full amount due is paid off, until then you are not eligible for the SBA loan.

If you are on an installment agreement with the IRS for taxes without any tax lien, you are in good standing.

Tip
Check with your Secretary of State, their Revenue Department can let you know if you have any outstanding tax lien in your name or in your business name.

Judgments: You can't have an open or outstanding judgment when you apply for the loan. The court's decision must have been satisfied for you to remain eligible for the SBA loan.

Settlements: A debt settlement is an agreement to debt reduction between the borrower and lender. Any account settled for less than the full original balance can be either an auto decline for lenders or if it was more than 1 or 2 years, it might be ok for some lenders.

Repossessions: If you have been delinquent on your mortgage payments, the creditor can repossess (take possession) your property. It can be an auto decline for lenders or it might be ok depending on a minimum timeframe from when it occurred.

Garnishments: When your wages are seized by court order to satisfy a debt you owe to a plaintiff creditor that you failed to pay. This is most likely a hard decline for your SBA loan application.

Chapter Two

Check your financials

Right on! You have now a good knowledge of your credit report and you know how to get your score to its best number! You are in control of your score, you have the power! Ok, let's move to the next step.

In this section, we will review how to read and understand your business financials and how to do simple formulas to know your business' profitability. How does that sound? Boring? Complicated? Well relax. My goal is to make it simple, easy and believe me I can make it fun! **This section is not a "must do" for you to apply for the SBA loan.** It is up to the lender to check the financials and evaluate if your business' profits are sufficient to repay the loan. For this guide, I find it useful to provide this section, as it is a big part of an application. Basically, the lender wants to know: Are the business financials good or bad? If a business is failing with constant losses, there is sadly no loan.

If you choose to skip this section, no worry at all, just jump to "Chapter Three: Gather your documents", page 59.

Note there can be different analysis methods, I will explain the most popular one among lenders.

I will indicate the documents necessary and then explain how to calculate your **business** debt service coverage ratio and your **global** debt service coverage ratio (business and personal). **I know these words all together might be scary if you never heard them before, but don't be afraid, simple definitions and examples are going to make it so easy.**

I. Business Financials Statements

Before we explain how to calculate the profitability of your business, we must know which documents to look at and how to read them properly. As a small business owner, you might delegate the "fun" financial paperwork part to an accountant, a bookkeeper or a CPA. Whether you or someone else prepares your financial statements and your taxes, it is important to have handy a few documents before you apply for an SBA loan. I will guide you here which parts of the documents and which numbers you need to focus on.

A. Profit and Loss

This statement measures a business' sales, costs and expenses during a specific period, usually a fiscal year or quarter. The purpose is to find the net profit of a company by subtracting the total expenses from the total revenue of that company.

On a P&L, you will see usually four to five sections:

- Revenue
- Cost of Goods Sold
- Expenses
- Other Incomes or Expenses (misc. categories)
- Net income (loss)

In each section, there are sub-categories, that the underwriter will look carefully, see if it makes sense with your industry.

The **Revenue** can come from either sale of products or services rendered or both.

The **Cost of Goods Sold** represents the direct costs of production for the company or the cost of delivering a service. It indicates how much it costs to purchase the materials used in the product and to pay for the labor to produce the good or to deliver the service. The revenue minus the Cost of Goods Sold will provide the Gross Profit.

In **Expenses**, you will find all the business operating expenses for its activity, like utilities, insurance, payroll if you have employees, rent if you rent a location, advertising, office supplies, permits and licenses, vehicle expenses, etc....You also find specifics expenses that will be used later to calculate your business profitability ratio: Depreciation, Amortization, Interests, Officer (owner) compensation.

Profit and Loss
January to December 2017

Revenue:

Gross Sales	$150 000,00
Less: Sales Returns and Allowances	$0,00
Net Sales	$150 000,00

Cost of Goods Sold:

Purchases	$16 000,00	
Freight-in	$5 000,00	
Direct Labor	$8 000,00	
Indirect Expenses	$0,00	
	$29 000,00	
Cost of Goods Sold		$29 000,00
Gross Profit (Loss)		$121 000,00

Expenses:

Advertising	$7 000,00	
Amortization	$400,00	
Bad Debts	$0,00	
Bank Charges	$225,00	
Charitable Contributions	$0,00	
Commissions	$0,00	
Contract Labor	$9 000,00	
Credit Card Fees	$432,00	
Delivery Expenses	$896,00	
Depreciation	$1 000,00	
Dues and Subscriptions	$0,00	
Insurance	$12 000,00	
Interest	$1 587,00	
Maintenance	$500,00	
Office Expenses	$350,00	
Officer compensation	$15 000,00	
Operating Supplies	$865,00	
Payroll Taxes	$4 000,00	
Permits and Licenses	$743,00	
Postage	$245,00	
Professional Fees	$875,00	
Property Taxes	$0,00	
Rent	$12 000,00	
Repairs	$428,00	
Telephone	$569,00	
Travel	$3 600,00	
Utilities	$690,00	
Vehicle Expenses	$2 890,00	
Wages	$20 000,00	
Total Expenses		$95 295,00
Net Operating Income		$25 705,00

Other Income:

Gain (Loss) on Sale of Assets	$2 000,00	
Interest Income	$0,00	
Total Other Income		$2 000,00

Net Income (Loss)	$27 705,00

Some accountants add another section named **Other Income** (or **Other Expenses**), that are not operating expenses, operating revenue or that are not yet sub categorized. It can be the sale or purchase of assets, the returns on investments. Therefore, it can be positive or negative.

The **Net Income** is the final number, after you subtract all the Expenses from your Gross Profit, and add the other income or other expense if any.

Here are simple definitions of depreciation, amortization, interest and officer compensation:

Depreciation: It concerns tangibles assets (equipment, vehicles, …) When you purchase equipment, you won't see that expense on your profit and loss. As that asset is used over its lifetime, it is losing value you can expense that "depreciation" of the equipment over the years it will be used.

Amortization: It is an accounting entry like depreciation, but this one concerns only intangible assets (goodwill, patents…) It spreads the cost every year during that period the asset is useful.

Interest: Simply the interest paid over a certain period on the business' outstanding debt.

Officer compensation: What the owner is paying himself for his activity in his company. The business pays usually W2 wages to its owner.

B. Balance Sheet

The Balance Sheet is the financial position of a company at a specific point of time, indicating what the company owns and owes, and the amount invested by shareholders.

On a Balance Sheet, you will see two main sections:

- Assets: what the business owns
- Liabilities: what the business owes

The assets can be cash, accounts receivables, bank accounts, inventory, as well as fixed assets like land, building, equipment, fixtures, vehicles.

The liabilities are divided between short-term and long-term debts to creditors, and the equity of its shareholders which is money they have invested in the company since inception and earnings the company has retained.

Your balance sheet must always be balanced, which means this formula should apply:

TOTAL ASSETS = TOTAL LIABILITIES + TOTAL EQUITY

The most recent balance sheet should be provided. If your interim profit and loss ends in July, then the balance sheet should be dated July 31st of that year.

Balance sheet
Date

ASSETS	$	LIABILITIES	$
Current Assets		**Current Liabilities**	
Cash		Accounts payable	
Accounts receivable		Short-term notes	
Inventory		Current portion of long-term notes	
Temporary investment		Interest payable	
Prepaid expenses		Taxes payable	
Total Current Assets		Accrued payroll	
		Total Current Liabilities	
Fixed Assets		**Long-term Liabilities**	
Long-term investments		Mortgage	
Land		Other long-term liabilities	
Buildings		**Total Long-Term Liabilities**	
(less accumulated depreciation)			
Plant and equipment		**Shareholders' Equity**	
(less accumulated depreciation)		Capital stock	
Furniture and fixtures		Retained earnings	
(less accumulated depreciation)		**Total Shareholders' Equity**	
Total Net Fixed Assets			
TOTAL ASSETS		**TOTAL LIABILITIES AND EQUITY**	

C. Business tax returns

Your business tax returns will be needed for the last three years to verify how the business performed. We are not going to review page by page these whole documents. The tax return gives the final "P&L" numbers of your business for the given year, the numbers that have been filed with the IRS. Just know where to find the sections we saw on the P&L earlier, and some of the sub-categories like Depreciation, Interests, Amortization. I am going to show you where to find them.

You can highlight on your returns the numbers corresponding to the lines I have marked with arrows on the following samples. I indicated on each form where to find the total revenue or income, the Cost of Goods Sold

If your business tax return is a Schedule C on your personal tax return from 1040 (used by sole proprietorship or single member LLC), all the P&L numbers are on the Page #1 of that Schedule C. On page #2, it can show Amortization cost.

SCHEDULE C (Form 1040)

Department of the Treasury
Internal Revenue Service (99)

Profit or Loss From Business
(Sole Proprietorship)
▶ Information about Schedule C and its separate instructions is at *www.irs.gov/schedulec.*
▶ Attach to Form 1040, 1040NR, or 1041; partnerships generally must file Form 1065.

OMB No. 1545-0074

2016

Attachment
Sequence No. **09**

Name of proprietor | Social security number (SSN)

A Principal business or profession, including product or service (see instructions) | **B** Enter code from instructions ▶

C Business name. If no separate business name, leave blank. | **D** Employer ID number (EIN), (see instr.)

E Business address (including suite or room no.) ▶
City, town or post office, state, and ZIP code

F Accounting method: **(1)** ☐ Cash **(2)** ☐ Accrual **(3)** ☐ Other (specify) ▶

G Did you "materially participate" in the operation of this business during 2016? If "No," see instructions for limit on losses . ☐ Yes ☐ No

H If you started or acquired this business during 2016, check here . . . . ▶ ☐

I Did you make any payments in 2016 that would require you to file Form(s) 1099? (see instructions) . . . . ☐ Yes ☐ No

J If "Yes," did you or will you file required Forms 1099? . . . . ☐ Yes ☐ No

Part I Income

1	Gross receipts or sales. See instructions for line 1 and check the box if this income was reported to you on Form W-2 and the "Statutory employee" box on that form was checked . . . . ▶ ☐	1	
2	Returns and allowances	2	
3	Subtract line 2 from line 1	3	**Total revenue**
4	Cost of goods sold (from line 42)	4	**Cost of Goods Sold**
5	**Gross profit.** Subtract line 4 from line 3	5	
6	Other income, including federal and state gasoline or fuel tax credit or refund (see instructions) . . .	6	
7	**Gross income.** Add lines 5 and 6 . . . . ▶	7	

Part II Expenses. Enter expenses for business use of your home **only** on line 30.

8	Advertising	8		18	Office expense (see instructions)	18	
9	Car and truck expenses (see instructions)	9		19	Pension and profit-sharing plans .	19	
				20	Rent or lease (see instructions):		
10	Commissions and fees .	10		a	Vehicles, machinery, and equipment	20a	
11	Contract labor (see instructions)	11		b	Other business property . . .	20b	
12	Depletion	12		21	Repairs and maintenance . . .	21	
13	Depreciation and section 179 expense deduction (not included in Part III) (see instructions). . . .	13	**Depreciation**	22	Supplies (not included in Part III) .	22	
				23	Taxes and licenses	23	
				24	Travel, meals, and entertainment:		
14	Employee benefit programs (other than on line 19). .	14		a	Travel	24a	
15	Insurance (other than health)	15		b	Deductible meals and entertainment (see instructions) .	24b	
16	Interest:			25	Utilities	25	
a	Mortgage (paid to banks, etc.)	16a	**Total interest**	26	Wages (less employment credits) .	26	
b	Other	16b	**=16a+16b**	27a	Other expenses (from line 48) . .	27a	
17	Legal and professional services	17		b	**Reserved for future use** . . .	27b	

28	**Total expenses** before expenses for business use of home. Add lines 8 through 27a . . . . . . ▶	28	**Total Expenses**
29	Tentative profit or (loss). Subtract line 28 from line 7	29	
30	Expenses for business use of your home. Do not report these expenses elsewhere. Attach Form 8829 unless using the simplified method (see instructions). **Simplified method filers only:** enter the total square footage of: (a) your home: _____ and (b) the part of your home used for business: _____ . Use the Simplified Method Worksheet in the instructions to figure the amount to enter on line 30	30	
31	**Net profit or (loss).** Subtract line 30 from line 29. • If a profit, enter on both **Form 1040, line 12** (or **Form 1040NR, line 13**) and on **Schedule SE, line 2.** (If you checked the box on line 1, see instructions). Estates and trusts, enter on **Form 1041, line 3.** • If a loss, you **must** go to line 32.	31	
32	If you have a loss, check the box that describes your investment in this activity (see instructions). • If you checked 32a, enter the loss on both **Form 1040, line 12,** (or **Form 1040NR, line 13**) and on **Schedule SE, line 2.** (If you checked the box on line 1, see the line 31 instructions). Estates and trusts, enter on **Form 1041, line 3.** • If you checked 32b, you **must** attach Form 6198. Your loss may be limited.	32a ☐ All investment is at risk. 32b ☐ Some investment is not at risk.

For Paperwork Reduction Act Notice, see the separate instructions. | Cat. No. 11334P | Schedule C (Form 1040) 2016

Schedule C (Form 1040) 2016   Page **2**

Part III **Cost of Goods Sold** (see instructions)

33 Method(s) used to
    value closing inventory: **a** ☐ Cost **b** ☐ Lower of cost or market **c** ☐ Other (attach explanation)

34 Was there any change in determining quantities, costs, or valuations between opening and closing inventory?
    If "Yes," attach explanation . . . . ☐ **Yes** ☐ **No**

35	Inventory at beginning of year. If different from last year's closing inventory, attach explanation . . .	35	
36	Purchases less cost of items withdrawn for personal use	36	
37	Cost of labor. Do not include any amounts paid to yourself	37	
38	Materials and supplies	38	
39	Other costs	39	
40	Add lines 35 through 39	40	
41	Inventory at end of year	41	
42	**Cost of goods sold.** Subtract line 41 from line 40. Enter the result here and on line 4	42	

Part IV **Information on Your Vehicle.** Complete this part **only** if you are claiming car or truck expenses on line 9 and are not required to file Form 4562 for this business. See the instructions for line 13 to find out if you must file Form 4562.

43 When did you place your vehicle in service for business purposes? (month, day, year) ▶ ___ / ___ / ___

44 Of the total number of miles you drove your vehicle during 2016, enter the number of miles you used your vehicle for:

a Business _____ **b** Commuting (see instructions) _____ **c** Other _____

45 Was your vehicle available for personal use during off-duty hours? . . . . ☐ **Yes** ☐ **No**

46 Do you (or your spouse) have another vehicle available for personal use?. . . . . ☐ **Yes** ☐ **No**

47a Do you have evidence to support your deduction? . . . . ☐ **Yes** ☐ **No**

 b If "Yes," is the evidence written? . . . . ☐ **Yes** ☐ **No**

Part V **Other Expenses.** List below business expenses not included on lines 8–26 or line 30.

This is where Amortization would be listed if you have any.	
48 **Total other expenses.** Enter here and on line 27a	48	

Schedule C (Form 1040) 2016

If your business tax return is a form 1120S (used by LLC or S-Corporation), or form 1120 (used by C-Corporation), you will find the P&L numbers on the Page #1 of that form.

Form 1120S

Department of the Treasury
Internal Revenue Service

U.S. Income Tax Return for an S Corporation

▶ Do not file this form unless the corporation has filed or is attaching Form 2553 to elect to be an S corporation.
▶ Information about Form 1120S and its separate instructions is at *www.irs.gov/form1120s.*

OMB No. 1545-0123

2016

For calendar year 2016 or tax year beginning , 2016, ending , 20

A S election effective date			D Employer identification number
B Business activity code number (see instructions)	TYPE OR PRINT	Name / Number, street, and room or suite no. If a P.O. box, see instructions. / City or town, state or province, country, and ZIP or foreign postal code	E Date incorporated / F Total assets (see instructions) $
C Check if Sch. M-3 attached ☐			

G Is the corporation electing to be an S corporation beginning with this tax year? ☐ Yes ☐ No   If "Yes," attach Form 2553 if not already filed

H Check if: (1) ☐ Final return (2) ☐ Name change (3) ☐ Address change (4) ☐ Amended return (5) ☐ S election termination or revocation

I Enter the number of shareholders who were shareholders during any part of the tax year . . . . . . ▶

Caution: Include **only** trade or business income and expenses on lines 1a through 21. See the instructions for more information.

Income

1a	Gross receipts or sales.	1a	
b	Returns and allowances	1b	
c	Balance. Subtract line 1b from line 1a	1c	**Revenue 1c**
2	Cost of goods sold (attach Form 1125-A)	2	**Cost of Goods Sold**
3	Gross profit. Subtract line 2 from line 1c	3	
4	Net gain (loss) from Form 4797, line 17 (attach Form 4797)	4	
5	Other income (loss) (see instructions—attach statement)	5	**Revenue 5**
6	Total income (loss). Add lines 3 through 5 ▶	6	

Total revenue = 1c + 5

Deductions (see instructions for limitations)

7	Compensation of officers (see instructions—attach Form 1125-E)	7	**Officers compensation**
8	Salaries and wages (less employment credits)	8	
9	Repairs and maintenance	9	
10	Bad debts	10	
11	Rents	11	
12	Taxes and licenses	12	
13	Interest	13	**Interest**
14	Depreciation not claimed on Form 1125-A or elsewhere on return (attach Form 4562)	14	**Depreciation**
15	Depletion (**Do not deduct oil and gas depletion.**)	15	
16	Advertising	16	
17	Pension, profit-sharing, etc., plans	17	
18	Employee benefit programs	18	
19	Other deductions (attach statement)	19	
20	Total deductions. Add lines 7 through 19 ▶	20	**Total Expenses**
21	Ordinary business income (loss). Subtract line 20 from line 6	21	

Tax and Payments

22a	Excess net passive income or LIFO recapture tax (see instructions)	22a		
b	Tax from Schedule D (Form 1120S)	22b		
c	Add lines 22a and 22b (see instructions for additional taxes)		22c	
23a	2016 estimated tax payments and 2015 overpayment credited to 2016	23a		
b	Tax deposited with Form 7004	23b		
c	Credit for federal tax paid on fuels (attach Form 4136)	23c		
d	Add lines 23a through 23c		23d	
24	Estimated tax penalty (see instructions). Check if Form 2220 is attached ▶ ☐		24	
25	Amount owed. If line 23d is smaller than the total of lines 22c and 24, enter amount owed		25	
26	Overpayment. If line 23d is larger than the total of lines 22c and 24, enter amount overpaid		26	
27	Enter amount from line 26 Credited to 2017 estimated tax ▶	Refunded ▶	27	

Under penalties of perjury, I declare that I have examined this return, including accompanying schedules and statements, and to the best of my knowledge and belief, it is true, correct, and complete. Declaration of preparer (other than taxpayer) is based on all information of which preparer has any knowledge.

Sign Here

▶ Signature of officer   Date   ▶ Title

May the IRS discuss this return with the preparer shown below (see instructions)? ☐ Yes ☐ No

Paid Preparer Use Only

Print/Type preparer's name	Preparer's signature	Date	Check ☐ if self-employed	PTIN
Firm's name ▶			Firm's EIN ▶	
Firm's address ▶			Phone no.	

For Paperwork Reduction Act Notice, see separate instructions.   Cat. No. 11510H   Form **1120S** (2016)

42

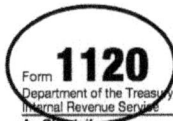

Form **1120**	**U.S. Corporation Income Tax Return**	OMB No. 1545-0123
Department of the Treasury Internal Revenue Service	For calendar year 2016 or tax year beginning _____ , 2016, ending _____ , 20 ___ ▶ Information about Form 1120 and its separate instructions is at *www.irs.gov/form1120.*	**2016**

A Check if:
1a Consolidated return (attach Form 851) ☐
b Life/nonlife consoli-dated return . . ☐
2 Personal holding co. (attach Sch. PH) . ☐
3 Personal service corp. (see instructions) . ☐
4 Schedule M-3 attached ☐

TYPE OR PRINT

Name

Number, street, and room or suite no. If a P.O. box, see instructions.

City or town, state, or province, country, and ZIP or foreign postal code

B Employer identification number

C Date incorporated

D Total assets (see instructions)
$

E Check if: (1) ☐ Initial return (2) ☐ Final return (3) ☐ Name change (4) ☐ Address change

Income

1a	Gross receipts or sales	1a	
b	Returns and allowances	1b	
c	Balance. Subtract line 1b from line 1a	1c	**Revenue 1c**
2	Cost of goods sold (attach Form 1125-A)	2	**Cost of Goods Sold**
3	Gross profit. Subtract line 2 from line 1c	3	
4	Dividends (Schedule C, line 19)	4	
5	Interest	5	
6	Gross rents	6	
7	Gross royalties	7	
8	Capital gain net income (attach Schedule D (Form 1120))	8	
9	Net gain or (loss) from Form 4797, Part II, line 17 (attach Form 4797) .	9	
10	Other income (see instructions—attach statement)	10	**Revenue 10**
11	**Total income.** Add lines 3 through 10 . . . . ▶	11	

Total revenue = 1c + 10

Deductions (See instructions for limitations on deductions.)

12	Compensation of officers (see instructions—attach Form 1125-E) . . . ▶	12	**Officers compensation**
13	Salaries and wages (less employment credits)	13	
14	Repairs and maintenance	14	
15	Bad debts	15	
16	Rents	16	
17	Taxes and licenses	17	
18	Interest	18	**Interest**
19	Charitable contributions	19	
20	Depreciation from Form 4562 not claimed on Form 1125-A or elsewhere on return (attach Form 4562) . .	20	**Depreciation**
21	Depletion	21	
22	Advertising	22	
23	Pension, profit-sharing, etc., plans	23	
24	Employee benefit programs	24	
25	Domestic production activities deduction (attach Form 8903)	25	
26	Other deductions (attach statement)	26	
27	**Total deductions.** Add lines 12 through 26 . . . . ▶	27	**Total Expenses**
28	Taxable income before net operating loss deduction and special deductions. Subtract line 27 from line 11.	28	
29a	Net operating loss deduction (see instructions)	29a	
b	Special deductions (Schedule C, line 20)	29b	
c	Add lines 29a and 29b	29c	

Tax, Refundable Credits, and Payments

30	**Taxable income.** Subtract line 29c from line 28. See instructions	30	
31	Total tax (Schedule J, Part I, line 11)	31	***Fed Income Tax**
32	Total payments and refundable credits (Schedule J, Part II, line 21) . . .	32	
33	Estimated tax penalty. See instructions. Check if Form 2220 is attached . . ▶ ☐	33	
34	**Amount owed.** If line 32 is smaller than the total of lines 31 and 33, enter amount owed . . .	34	
35	**Overpayment.** If line 32 is larger than the total of lines 31 and 33, enter amount overpaid . .	35	
36	Enter amount from line 35 you want: **Credited to 2017 estimated tax ▶**	Refunded ▶	36	

Sign Here

Under penalties of perjury, I declare that I have examined this return, including accompanying schedules and statements, and to the best of my knowledge and belief, it is true, correct, and complete. Declaration of preparer (other than taxpayer) is based on all information of which preparer has any knowledge.

▶ _____ Signature of officer   Date   ▶ _____ Title

May the IRS discuss this return with the preparer shown below? See instructions. ☐ Yes ☐ No

Paid Preparer Use Only

Print/Type preparer's name	Preparer's signature	Date	Check ☐ if self-employed	PTIN
Firm's name ▶			Firm's EIN ▶	
Firm's address ▶			Phone no.	

For Paperwork Reduction Act Notice, see separate instructions.   Cat. No. 11450Q   Form **1120** (2016)

If your business tax return is a form 1065 (used by Partnership), you will find the P&L numbers on the Page #1. There is no "officers' compensation" in partnerships, but "guaranteed payments to partners", just different vocabulary used for the compensation to the business' partners.

For business tax returns 1120S, 1120 and 1065, the Amortization expense is either on a separate statement page or is on "form 4562" pages of the tax returns (see below).

Form 4562 (2016)   Page **2**

Part V   **Listed Property** (Include automobiles, certain other vehicles, certain aircraft, certain computers, and property used for entertainment, recreation, or amusement.)

Note: For any vehicle for which you are using the standard mileage rate or deducting lease expense, complete **only** 24a, 24b, columns (a) through (c) of Section A, all of Section B, and Section C if applicable.

Section A—Depreciation and Other Information (Caution: See the instructions for limits for passenger automobiles.**)**

24a Do you have evidence to support the business/investment use claimed? ☐ Yes ☐ No   **24b** If "Yes," is the evidence written? ☐ Yes ☐ No

(a) Type of property (list vehicles first)	(b) Date placed in service	(c) Business/ investment use percentage	(d) Cost or other basis	(e) Basis for depreciation (business/investment use only)	(f) Recovery period	(g) Method/ Convention	(h) Depreciation deduction	(i) Elected section 179 cost
25 Special depreciation allowance for qualified listed property placed in service during the tax year and used more than 50% in a qualified business use (see instructions) .				**25**				
26 Property used more than 50% in a qualified business use:								
		%						
		%						
		%						
27 Property used 50% or less in a qualified business use:								
		%				S/L –		
		%				S/L –		
		%				S/L –		
28 Add amounts in column (h), lines 25 through 27. Enter here and on line 21, page 1 .				**28**				
29 Add amounts in column (i), line 26. Enter here and on line 7, page 1							**29**	

Section B—Information on Use of Vehicles

Complete this section for vehicles used by a sole proprietor, partner, or other "more than 5% owner," or related person. If you provided vehicles to your employees, first answer the questions in Section C to see if you meet an exception to completing this section for those vehicles.

	(a) Vehicle 1		(b) Vehicle 2		(c) Vehicle 3		(d) Vehicle 4		(e) Vehicle 5		(f) Vehicle 6	
30 Total business/investment miles driven during the year (**don't** include commuting miles) .												
31 Total commuting miles driven during the year												
32 Total other personal (noncommuting) miles driven												
33 Total miles driven during the year. Add lines 30 through 32												
34 Was the vehicle available for personal use during off-duty hours?	Yes	No	Yes	No	Yes	No	Yes	No	Yes	No	Yes	No
35 Was the vehicle used primarily by a more than 5% owner or related person? . .												
36 Is another vehicle available for personal use?												

Section C—Questions for Employers Who Provide Vehicles for Use by Their Employees

Answer these questions to determine if you meet an exception to completing Section B for vehicles used by employees who **aren't** more than 5% owners or related persons (see instructions).

	Yes	No
37 Do you maintain a written policy statement that prohibits all personal use of vehicles, including commuting, by your employees?		
38 Do you maintain a written policy statement that prohibits personal use of vehicles, except commuting, by your employees? See the instructions for vehicles used by corporate officers, directors, or 1% or more owners . .		
39 Do you treat all use of vehicles by employees as personal use?		
40 Do you provide more than five vehicles to your employees, obtain information from your employees about the use of the vehicles, and retain the information received?		
41 Do you meet the requirements concerning qualified automobile demonstration use? (See instructions		

Amortization will show here.

Part VI   **Amortization**

(a) Description of costs	(b) Date amortization begins	(c) Amortizable amount	(d) Code section	(e) Amortization period or percentage	(f) Amortization for this year
42 Amortization of costs that begins during your 2016 tax year (see instructions):					
43 Amortization of costs that began before your 2016 tax year				**43**	
44 Total. Add amounts in column (f). See the instructions for where to report				**44**	

Form **4562** (2016)

Now that we have reviewed the financial documents and know where to find profit and loss items, let's do the math!

II. Business Debt Service Coverage Ratio

Lenders will lend money only to profitable businesses. The lenders won't lend to a business facing declining trends and huge losses which could potentially lead to default. They will look back at the last three years of your business financials to analyze its trends, as well as the interim period (from the end of your last fiscal year to the most recent month when you applied).

Example: If your business tax year ends December 31st each year, and you apply for a loan in August 2018. You will have 2015, 2016 and 2017 as full taxed year, and the lender will request to see your financial from January 2018 to at least end of June or July 2018, that will be the "interim period".

To study if a business is profitable and will be able to repay the SBA loan, lenders will use a ratio of profitability. **It is the ratio of cash the business has available to pay its debt.**

The ratio is known as the Debt Service Coverage Ratio. Don't be afraid about the vocabulary here, the following paragraphs will explain it all in an easy and simple manner.

We will review this ratio on two levels: first the Business DSCR (Debt Service Coverage Ratio) and secondly the Global DSCR (Debt Service Coverage Ratio).

- **Business DSCR** is the measure of cash available in your business to pay its current debt obligations.
- **Global DSCR** is the measure of cash available in your business and in your own "pocket" as an individual to pay the business debt obligations and your personal debt obligations.

The first one concerns only the business entity, while the global ratio also involves your personal income and debt, as an individual. Ratios are calculated on a full year. We will explain later how to calculate the business ratio of the interim period when the year is not yet complete.

Each lender can set their minimum Business and Global DSCR, **usually 1.15 or 1.25 is the minimum** required.

A. How to calculate your Business DSCR

Business DSCR will be found by dividing the business earnings (specifically EBITDA) made on a year by its annual debt payment.

EBITDA = Earnings Before Interests, Taxes, Depreciation, Amortization

We need to find out first the Earnings the business made on a full year, before Interest (on its debt), Taxes, Depreciation, and Amortization.

The EBITDA is a good measure of how much cash profit a company made in each year, it is an effective indicator of a company's financial health. It indicates how a company performs without the need to consider taxes, financial decisions, or accounting decisions.

To find out the EBITDA you simply take your net profit and add back interest expense, taxes, depreciation, amortization if any and the officer compensation if any.

If you paid yourself wages (you are on W2 from your own company) and it shows as an expense line in your P&L statement, add back your own officer compensation. The reason is these wages represent part of your business' profit, it needs to be accounted in the company total earnings.

Let's practice finding the EBITDA on an example. I will use a yearly Profit and Loss statement example but you can do the same thing with your yearly tax returns. I showed you the pages and items to look at earlier, the items are named the same, they are just in a tax return format.

Case study #1:

Next page is a full year P&L (profit and loss) sample.

1. Pick the **Net Income** number at the bottom of the document profit and loss, the very last one. In our example it is **$27,705**.

2. Now add back the Interest, the Taxes if any, the Depreciation and Amortization if any, and officer compensation if any. In our example there is no tax expense, but Interest is $1,587, Depreciation is $1,000 and Amortization is $400. If you paid yourself wages, and expensed these wages in the expenses column, you can add them back as well. Here in our example we can add back the officer compensation $15,000. **Total add back** = 1,587+1,000+400+15,000= **$17,987**.

3. **EBITDA = Net income + Add back**
   = $27,705 + $17,987
   = $45,692.

Do the same on your own P&L and note down your EBITDA.

Profit and Loss
January to December 2017

Revenue:

Gross Sales	$150 000,00
Less: Sales Returns and Allowances	$0,00
Net Sales	$150 000,00

Cost of Goods Sold:

Purchases	$16 000,00	
Freight-in	$5 000,00	
Direct Labor	$8 000,00	
Indirect Expenses	$0,00	
	$29 000,00	
Cost of Goods Sold		$29 000,00
Gross Profit (Loss)		$121 000,00

Expenses:

Advertising	$7 000,00	
Amortization	$400,00	
Bad Debts	$0,00	
Bank Charges	$225,00	
Charitable Contributions	$0,00	
Commissions	$0,00	
Contract Labor	$9 000,00	
Credit Card Fees	$432,00	
Delivery Expenses	$896,00	
Depreciation	$1 000,00	
Dues and Subscriptions	$0,00	
Insurance	$12 000,00	
Interest	$1 587,00	
Maintenance	$500,00	
Office Expenses	$350,00	
Officer compensation	$15 000,00	
Operating Supplies	$865,00	
Payroll Taxes	$4 000,00	
Permits and Licenses	$743,00	
Postage	$245,00	
Professional Fees	$875,00	
Property Taxes	$0,00	
Rent	$12 000,00	
Repairs	$428,00	
Telephone	$569,00	
Travel	$3 600,00	
Utilities	$690,00	
Vehicle Expenses	$2 890,00	
Wages	$20 000,00	
Total Expenses		$95 295,00
Net Operating Income		$25 705,00

Other Income:

Gain (Loss) on Sale of Assets	$2 000,00	
Interest Income	$0,00	
Total Other Income		$2 000,00

Net Income (Loss)		$27 705,00

You can do the same calculations with your business tax return. Look at the next page example on form 1120S, you can find out the same items on other business tax returns forms.

- Step 1 you calculate the **Total revenue**

- Step 2 you calculate the **Net Income**

- Step 3 you calculate the **EBITDA**

U.S. Income Tax Return for an S Corporation

Form **1120S**

► Do not file this form unless the corporation has filed or is attaching Form 2553 to elect to be an S corporation.
► Information about Form 1120S and its separate instructions is at *www.irs.gov/form1120s*.

OMB No. 1545-0123

2016

Department of the Treasury
Internal Revenue Service

For calendar year 2016 or tax year beginning _____ , 2016, ending _____ , 20 _____

A S election effective date	**TYPE OR PRINT** Name	**D** Employer identification number
B Business activity code number (see instructions)	Number, street, and room or suite no. If a P.O. box, see instructions.	**E** Date incorporated
C Check if Sch. M-3 attached ☐	City or town, state or province, country, and ZIP or foreign postal code	**F** Total assets (see instructions) $

G Is the corporation electing to be an S corporation beginning with this tax year? ☐ Yes ☐ No   If "Yes," attach Form 2553 if not already filed

H Check if: **(1)** ☐ Final return **(2)** ☐ Name change **(3)** ☐ Address change **(4)** ☐ Amended return **(5)** ☐ S election termination or revocation

I Enter the number of shareholders who were shareholders during any part of the tax year . . . . ►

Caution: Include **only** trade or business income and expenses on lines 1a through 21. See the instructions for more information.

Income

1a	Gross receipts or sales 1a	150000	
b	Returns and allowances 1b	0	
c	Balance. Subtract line 1b from line 1a . ① . . . . ►	1c	150000
2	Cost of goods sold (attach Form 1125-A) .	2	29000
3	Gross profit. Subtract line 2 from line 1c .	3	
4	Net gain (loss) from Form 4797, line 17 (att	4	
5	Other income (loss) (see instructions—attach statement)	5	2000
6	**Total income (loss).** Add lines 3 through 5 . . . . ►	6	

Total revenue =1c + 5 = 150,000 + 2,000 = 152,000

Deductions (see instructions for limitations)

7	Compensation of officers (see instructions—attach Form 1125-E)	7	15000
8	Salaries and wages (less employment credits)	8	
9	Repairs and maintenance	9	
10	Bad debts	10	
11	Rents	11	
12	Taxes and licenses	12	
13	Interest	13	1587
14	Depreciation not claimed on Form 1125-A or elsewhere on return (attach Form 4562) . . .	14	1000
15	Depletion **(Do not deduct oil and gas depletion.)**	15	
		16	
		17	
		18	
19	Other deductions (attach statement)	19	77708
20	**Total deductions.** Add lines 7 through 19 . . . . ►	20	95295
21	**Ordinary business income (loss).** Subtract line 20 from line 6	21	
22a	Excess net passive income or LIFO recapture tax (see instructions) . . 22a		

Let's pretend here the page 2 of form 4562 for other deductions shows Amortization for $400.

② **NET INCOME**
= Total revenue - Cost of Goods Sold - Total deductions
= 152,000 - 29,000 - 95,295
= 27,705

③ **EBITDA**
= NET INCOME + Interests + Depreciation + Amortization + Officer Compensation
= 27,705 + 1,587 + 1,000 + 400 + 15,000
= $45,692

ANNUAL DEBT PAYMENT

All existing debts in the name of the business need to be accounted for. The lender will also add to these debts the estimated SBA loan monthly payment.

To help you stay organized and not leave out any debts, use this sample Business Debt Schedule below and list all the debts in the business name.

Example:

Name of lender	Type of debt (credit card, line of credit, term loan, cash advance…)	Origination date (year, month if known)	Outstanding balance	Minimum monthly payment	Months remaining (if any)	Refinanced by the SBA Loan? Y/N
Lender A	Term Loan	October 2009	$35,860	$427	84	N
Lender B	Credit card	May 2012	$8,300	$250	n/a	N
Lender C	Cash advance	June 2016	$12,000	$1,000	12	Y
Name of lender	Type of debt (credit card, line of credit, term loan, cash advance…)	Origination date (year, month if known)	Outstanding balance	Minimum monthly payment	Months remaining (if any)	Refinanced by the SBA Loan? Y/N

Tip

Do not omit any debt, as you need to be fully honest and accurate. If the lenders find out later stage another debt not disclosed, it might ruin your application, as the ratio has been wrongly calculated.

Make sure you do not list debts that are personal, this is only for the debts in the business name. If you are refinancing one or several business debts with the SBA loan, indicate so on the far-right column. Refinanced debts must be listed for transparent disclosure; but in the calculation of course we won't count them since they will be replaced by the SBA loan. Once you have written down ALL your business debts, find out the Total of your monthly payments for debts you are keeping (not the ones getting refinanced). Add to this number the SBA loan monthly payment. Remember, we explained earlier, the lender will count the SBA loan payment to make sure the business can repay it. Multiply this total monthly payment amount by 12 which will give you the Total Annual Debt Payment of your business.

We are now able to find out the Business DSCR with the following formula:

> **Business DSRC = EBITDA / Total Annual Debt Payment (including the SBA loan)**

Case study #1:

A business is applying for $100,000 SBA Loan, with $1,160 monthly payment.

From the prior case study, we found out that this business' **EBITDA is $45,692**.

On the business debt schedule sample above, we have three debts examples. One is getting refinanced by the SBA loan (see Lender C debt, top right column says "Y" to be refinanced) so it will disappear and be replaced by the SBA loan monthly payment, and we will keep only two current debts that are not getting refinanced (the Lenders A and B debts stay):

1. Lender A debt $427/month,
2. Lender B debt $250/month,
3. to which we add the future SBA Loan debt $1,160/month.

Total monthly payment will be 427 + 250 + 1,160 = $1,837.

Therefore, the **total annual debt payment** is $1,837 x 12 months = **$22,044**.

Business DSCR = EBITDA / Total Annual Debt Payment
= 45,692 / 22,044
= **2.07**

In this study case #1 the Business DSCR is 2.07, which is a passing ratio!

Do the math and note down your Business DSCR. Each lender has its own minimum required, often between x and x. Therefore, in our example Case Study #1, we have a profitable and eligible business for these lenders, as the ratio is higher than the minimum required.

Interim period: You may wonder; how to calculate the Business DSCR **when the year is not completed yet**? Piece of cake! Let me show you how.

If your profit and loss is only a few months because the year is not yet finished, there is a way to calculate an annual Business DSCR. Let's say you have an interim period of 5 months, January up to May. We are going to annualize these 5 months to 12 months.

We need to calculate first the EBITDA of the 5 months' period. Then we will annualize that number on 12 months. It is a projection of a year based on only the few months passed. So, if your first 5 months are great; the year projection is going to look very good. If that's not the case; the 5 months turned out to be a very bad period, then the projection won't look good, but you can explain what happened.

Case study #2

Donald has a business applying for an SBA loan during summer. He provided the tax returns of the prior years and only has for the current year a profit and loss up to end of May. During these first 5 months of the year, called the interim period, Donald's business made the following:
- $70,000 in total revenue
- $15,000 in Cost of Goods Sold
- $45,000 in total deductions (total expenses)
    - including $1,000 in interests
    - including $450 in depreciation
    - including $170 in amortization
    - including $8,000 in officer compensation

Net Income = $70,000 - $15,000 - $45,000 = $10,000
EBITDA for the 5 months' period = $10,000 + $1,000 + $450 + $170 + $8,000 = $19,620
EBITDA annualized on 12 months = (EBITDA of 5 months / 5) x 12
$$= (\$19,620 / 5) \times 12$$
$$= \mathbf{\$47,088}$$

Let's say his business only has two debts; for which he pays $100 and $250 per month. The SBA loan monthly payment would be $1,400.
Total annual debt payment = ($100 + $250 + $1,400) x 12 = **$21,000**

Business DSCR = EBITDA / Total Annual Debt Payment
$$= \$47,088 / \$21,000$$
$$= \mathbf{2.24}$$

Donald can relax; his business' ratio for the interim period is passing with a great 2.24.

Now that we have worked on the Business ratio, let's explain how to calculate the Global DSCR (that ratio will included your personal finances as an individual).

B. How to calculate your Global DSCR

The Global DSCR will indicate if the guarantor financial situation is sufficient to handle the SBA loan payments.

The owner of the business will be a guarantor on the SBA loan. If there are multiple business owners, all owners having at least 20% of ownership will be a guarantor. Regarding a married couple owning a business together, even if one of the spouse has at least 5% of ownership, it makes him/her a guarantor as well.

Each guarantor needs to list:

- his annual income (wages, guaranteed payment, pensions if recurring, social security if recurring, IRA distributions if recurring each year, income from Schedule C from business other than the one applying for the SBA loan)

  - his annual rental real estate revenue, interests, depreciation and expenses if any.

  - his Federal Income Tax, its Real Estate Property Tax if any, its State Income Tax if any.

  - his mortgage(s) payment if any, or rent paid, its Home Equity Line of Credit if any.

  - his personal debts (minimum monthly payments due on ALL its personal debts like credit cards, personal loan, personal line of credit, student loan, auto loan, auto lease,)

You might ask: when spouses file jointly but only one of them owns 100% of the business, do we split or not the common income, debts or taxes?

The lenders can have different views on this, but most often they will only account the "spouse business owner" own debts, the couple's mortgage payment will be accounted in full, the rental real estate revenue and taxes would be accounted in full too. A common practice would be to account all the couple income and common debts and taxes, but to split the personal debts of each spouse and count only the business owner's personal debts.

Case study #3:

Guy, married filing jointly, owns 100% of its business. He owns his home with a mortgage and owns a rental property free and clear (no mortgage). His spouse earns $30,000 in wages from a part time job. Guy's EBITDA from his business is the one we calculated in Case #1, EBITDA was $45,692. Attention here, be careful to not double count income, his officer compensation of $15,000 is included already in the EBITDA of his business, therefore we are not adding it as personal income.

Let's complete these lines with money coming into Guy's household account (+) and money coming out of the household account (-) during a specific year. Here we have no rental real estate interests as the rental property is owned free and clear of mortgage.

	+	-
Guy's business EBITDA	$45,692	
Wages of John's spouse	$30,000	
Wages of John (his officer compensation)	Already accounted in the EBITDA (Do not double count these wages)	
Rental Real Estate Revenue	$12,000	
Rental Real Estate Interests	n/a	
Rental Real Estate Depreciation	$4,000	
Rental Real Estate Expenses		$5,000
Federal Income Tax		$9,000
Real Estate Property Tax		$6,000
State Tax		$2,000
Home mortgage ($850/month)		$10,200/year
Credit Card A (min $25/month)		$300/year
Credit Card B (min $100/month)		$1,200/year
Credit Card C (min $50/month)		$600/year
Auto loan ($300/month)		$3,600/year
TOTAL	$91,692	$37,900

The Global DSCR takes all the business EBITDA (earnings before interests, taxes, depreciation and amortization) and all the household's wages and income from real estate (interests and depreciation accounted as add backs), and divide it by the business debts and the guarantor's personal debts, as well as the SBA debt that they apply for.

The Global DSCR is calculated with the following formula:

Long version
Global DSCR = (business EBITDA + household personal incomes without the guarantor's wages from his business + real estate interest and depreciation if any) / (annual total business debt payment SBA loan included + annual guarantor personal debt payment + annual household taxes and real estate expenses if any)

Short version
Global DSCR = (EBITDA + total personal incomes) / (total business debt + total personal debt + taxes + real estate expenses)

So, from the Case #1 and #3 information we have the following numbers for Guy's business:
Business EBITDA = $45,692
Household personal income = $30,000 + $12,000 + $4,000 = $46,000
Annual total business debt payment = $22,044
Annual guarantor personal debt payment = $10,200 + $300 + $1,200 + $600 + $3,600= $15,900
Annual household taxes and real estate expenses = $5,000 + $9,000 + $6,000 + $2,000 = $22,000

Global DSCR	= ($45,692 + $46,000) / ($22,044 + $15,900 + $22,000)
	= $91,692 / $59,944
	= **1.53**

In this case study we do have a passing global ratio of 1.53, if we consider our lenders are looking for a global ratio above 1.15 or even 1.25. **Check your ratio now with your own numbers!**

Now that you checked your credit score and your financial eligibility to repay the loan, let's start to gather the documents that will be requested by the lender.

Chapter Three

Gather your documents

While it is often said that an SBA loan requires a mountain of documents and applicants can feel discouraged by the list, be mindful you have the power to speed up the process! Organized borrowers have been able to provide me all the documents and information in just three to five days. I got them funded five days later, so the whole process took maximum ten days! **Roll up your sleeves, you can do it!**

To help you in this journey, I will list the documentation and explain why each is needed and where to get it (if not in your computer's hard drive or hard paper copies in your desk!). Be aware your lender can ask for more documents related to your specific situation, depending on your case and the State you are in, but this list is the main documentation needed for most businesses across the United States.

I have attached three checklists depending on your business location status, pick the one best related to your situation:

1. Documents checklist for **business home** operated
2. Documents checklist for **business leasing** its location
3. Documents checklist for **business owning** its location

Documents Checklist – Home operated

Business:
- ☐ 3 last years' business tax returns
- ☐ Profit and loss interim period
- ☐ Balance sheet dated end of interim period
- ☐ Business debts schedule
- ☐ Assets list *(if business owns vehicle(s) in its name: copy of the vehicle(s) title + certificate of insurance)*
- ☐ Articles of incorporation or organization
- ☐ Operating Agreement or By-Laws or Partnership Agreement
- ☐ Certificate of good standing or "Active Status"
- ☐ DBA current certificate if any
- ☐ Copy of a voided business check and/or Wire instructions from your bank
- ☐ Business trends explanation

Location:
- ☐ Proof of home ownership
- ☐ Home mortgage last statement
- ☐ Pictures of your home office/desk area

Insurance:
- ☐ General Liability
- ☐ Business Personal Property (or Home owner insurance if business assets are less than $5,000)
- ☐ Worker compensation (if required by your State)
- ☐ Malpractice insurance (if any)

Per guarantor:
- ☐ Color photo of your driver license
- ☐ 3 last years' individual tax returns
- ☐ Most recent pay stub or W2 (if any)
- ☐ Credit report explanation
- ☐ Form 413 to complete
- ☐ Form 1919 to complete
- ☐ Form G-845 + copy of Green Card (only if non US citizen)

Debts to refinance

If loan/line of credit/merchant cash advance
- ☐ Promissory note
- ☐ 12 months of payment history
- ☐ Payoff quote

If Credit card:
- ☐ Last 12 months of credit card statements

Equipment to purchase:
- ☐ Invoice for the equipment
- ☐ Wire instructions of the merchant

Affiliate(s) = Other Business owned by guarantor(s):
- ☐ Affiliate form

Note: Each business being different, additional documents/clarifications may be requested after further review, to help your application remain eligible per the SBA lender requirements.

Documents Checklist – Lease location

Business:
- ☐ 3 last years' business tax returns
- ☐ Profit and loss interim period
- ☐ Balance sheet dated end of interim period
- ☐ Business debts schedule
- ☐ Assets list *(if business owns vehicle(s) in its name: copy of the vehicle(s) title + certificate of insurance)*
- ☐ Articles of incorporation or organization
- ☐ Operating Agreement or By-Laws or Partnership Agreement
- ☐ Certificate of good standing or "Active Status"
- ☐ DBA current certificate if any
- ☐ Copy of a voided business check and/or Wire instructions from your bank
- ☐ Business trends explanation

Location:
- ☐ Commercial lease agreement plus any amendments
- ☐ Landlord Subordination agreement (to be provided by lender)
- ☐ Option to renew (to be provided by lender)

Insurance:
- ☐ General Liability
- ☐ Business Personal Property
- ☐ Worker compensation (if required by your State)
- ☐ Malpractice insurance (if any)

Per guarantor:
- ☐ Color photo of your driver license
- ☐ 3 last years' individual tax returns
- ☐ Most recent pay stub or W2 (if any)
- ☐ Credit report explanation
- ☐ Form 413 to complete
- ☐ Form 1919 to complete
- ☐ Form G-845 + copy of Green Card (only if non US citizen)

Debts to refinance

If loan/line of credit/merchant cash advance
- ☐ Promissory note
- ☐ 12 months of payment history
- ☐ Payoff quote
If Credit card:
- ☐ Last 12 months of credit card statements

Equipment to purchase:
- ☐ Invoice for the equipment
- ☐ Wire instructions of the merchant

Affiliate(s) = Other Business owned by guarantor(s):
- ☐ Affiliate form

Note: Each business being different, additional documents/clarifications may be requested after further review, to help your application remain eligible per the SBA lender requirements.

Documents Checklist – Owned location

Business:
- ☐ 3 last years' business tax returns
- ☐ Profit and loss interim period
- ☐ Balance sheet dated end of interim period
- ☐ Business debts schedule
- ☐ Assets list *(if business owns vehicle(s) in its name: copy of the vehicle(s) title + certificate of insurance)*
- ☐ Articles of incorporation or organization
- ☐ Operating Agreement or By-Laws or Partnership Agreement
- ☐ Certificate of good standing or "Active Status"
- ☐ DBA current certificate if any
- ☐ Copy of a voided business check and/or Wire instructions from your bank
- ☐ Business trends explanation

Location:
- ☐ Environmental questionnaire (to be provided by lender)
- ☐ Proof of commercial property ownership
- ☐ Most recent commercial mortgage statement (if any)
- ☐ Commercial lease agreement + any amendments between Landlord (if location owned by business owner himself or through an affiliate business) and Tenant (the applicant business)
- ☐ Landlord Subordination agreement (to be provided by lender)
- ☐ Option to renew (to be provided by lender)

Insurance:
- ☐ General Liability
- ☐ Business Personal Property (content + building)
- ☐ Worker compensation (if required by your State)
- ☐ Malpractice insurance (if any)

Per guarantor:
- ☐ Color photo of your driver license
- ☐ 3 last years' individual tax returns
- ☐ Most recent pay stub or W2 (if any)
- ☐ Credit report explanation
- ☐ Form 413 to complete
- ☐ Form 1919 to complete
- ☐ Form G-845 + copy of Green Card (only if non US citizen)

Debts to refinance

If loan/line of credit/merchant cash advance
- ☐ Promissory note
- ☐ 12 months of payment history
- ☐ Payoff quote
If Credit card:
- ☐ Last 12 months of credit card statements

Equipment to purchase:
- ☐ Invoice for the equipment
- ☐ Wire instructions of the merchant

Affiliate(s) = Other Business owned by guarantor(s):
- ☐ Affiliate form

Note: Each business being different, additional documents/clarifications may be requested after further review, to help your application remain eligible per the SBA lender requirements.

If your business has several locations, you will need to provide the locations related documents for each address and make sure the business insurance certificates covers all the addresses.

Let's explain below each item seen in these different checklists, concerning the following sections: business, insurance, location, guarantor, debts to refinance, equipment to purchase, affiliate (if any), what is it, why is it needed, where to find it.

I. Business

3 LAST YEARS OF BUSINESS TAX RETURNS

What is it: A business tax return is the document you file each year with the Internal Revenue Service (IRS) to report your business' income, profit and loss, deductions. Your business tax returns can be on the IRS forms 1120, 1120s, 1065 or it can be the Schedule C part of your personal tax returns. The choice of the form is depending on your legal business entity (sole proprietorship, partnership, corporation or s-corporation). Provide copy of the 3 returns that were indeed filed, not your drafts. Make sure to provide the full returns, with any Schedules and Statements available.

Why is it needed: The lender will assess the business profitability for the last three years. It gives precious information on how the business is managed, where the expenses went, how the income evolves, its assets, its liabilities (Schedule L), if the ownership percentage changed, if the business changed its name, its business address and its Employer Identification Number (EIN).
The forms 1120s and 1065 must include a Schedule K1 that shows the ownership structure. The form 1120 has the same on the Schedule G.

Where to find it: People usually keep them safely and securely at home. You can ask your CPA if he takes care of it for you. **If it was lost, you can ask for complete transcripts to be send by mail or fax, call your local IRS center or order them online on www.irs.gov** .

PROFIT AND LOSS FOR INTERIM PERIOD

What is it: This document is a financial statement, that summarizes the revenue and all the expenses of the business during a chosen period, could be a month or a quarter.

<u>Why is it needed</u>: To assess the business profitability during a period that has not been filed yet with the IRS. These numbers are subject to change slightly, due to adjustments when the business owner or CPA is filing the tax returns.

<u>Note</u>: If you are applying for an SBA loan early in the year, before filing is due for businesses, you will have the full last year not filed yet and 1 or 3 months of the current year during which you conducted business. Therefore, the lender won't be able to see the tax return for last year, you will be asked to provide a P&L for the full last year and a separate P&L for the first few months of the current year.

<u>Where to find it</u>: Yourself or an accountant probably use an accounting software like QuickBooks to keep track of the revenue and expenses along the year. You should be able to get the numbers easily for the most recent months. If your business does not have an accounting software, you can do it the old fashion way, by looking at your paper records (sales receipts, bills, purchases, banking account statements,) to compile the information and make your own Profit and Loss on a separate sheet.
Example: If you filed 2016 business tax returns, and you applied for an SBA loan in June 2017, you should print out a profit and loss for the interim period January 1st to end of April or May 2017.

BALANCE SHEET

<u>What is it</u>: This financial statement shows the assets, liabilities and capital of a business at a specific point of time.

<u>Why is it needed</u>: The lender will check what type of assets owns the business, its current value, as these would be the loan's collateral. In the same time, the lender can view the debts of the business that are still outstanding. They verify the accuracy of the balance sheet, if it is unbalanced they will work with the applicant and accountant to find out where is the error and adjust it with information that was incorrect or missing.

<u>Where to find it</u>: It is usually done with the same accounting software used for the profit and loss.

BUSINESS DEBT SCHEDULE (see appendix)

<u>What is it</u>: It lists all the business' debts outstanding.

<u>Why is it needed</u>: It helps speed up the application, showing on one document all the

debts with the following details: name of lender, type of credit, outstanding balance, minimum monthly payment, credit limit if any, months remaining if term loan, and interest percent. It clarifies which debts are going to be refinanced by the SBA loan.

Where to find it: In this book's appendix we provide you with a template for you to complete. You can make your own, the idea is to keep the same columns and list out all the debts in the business name.

ASSETS LIST* (see appendix)

What is it: It lists all the assets belonging to the business, used for its daily operations. Assets are computers, hardware, equipment, tools, furniture, appliances, machinery and vehicles in the business name.

Why is it needed: It provides a clear list of collateral for the lender. He will set a blanket lien on all of them and large items, vehicles or special machines with a high value, will usually get a lien on them, for the benefit of the SBA lender in case of default on the SBA loan. Blanket lien will give the right to seize all types of assets of the debtor in case of default.

Where to find it: A template is provided to you in this book, in the appendix. If you have not kept any written records of what your purchased for your business along the years, no worry, simply consider your business location (your office, shop, garage, storage, wherever is your place of business where you work from or store your business assets), and list out on the template what you have. Make sure to not forget business' assets that might be temporary held at a job site for example: bobcat for contractors. Give your best estimation of original and current market values. No need to overvalue your assets to "look good on collateral", the lender needs to make sure the total current value disclosed is enough covered by your insurance policy and to be the closest to real value of each asset if they must be sold tomorrow.

---

*IF YOUR BUSINESS OWNS VEHICLES IN ITS NAME (this does not include vehicles part of the inventory for sale of an auto shop for example)

VEHICLE CERTIFICATE OF TITLE (ORIGINAL OR COLOR COPY)

What is it: It is the proof of ownership of the vehicle and its current registration.

Why is it needed: If the business owns vehicles in its own name, whether used for delivery, services, or simply to drive to your work place, they will be part of the collateral assets for the lender who can put itself as lien holder if the vehicle is owned clear and free.

Where to find it: In your vehicle usually. If lost ask your local DMV.

VEHICLE CERTIFICATE OF INSURANCE

What is it: Proof of current insurance coverage of a vehicle. Comprehensive and collision coverage is required.

Why is it needed: To insure the vehicle will be covered (costs paid by the insurance) in case of damages caused by independent events (fire, natural disaster, vandalism, theft, etc.) and in case of damage due to the driver's action or car's condition (collision, repair costs, replacement costs).

Where to find it: Your insurance agent can provide that document, the SBA lender may ask if he is taking a lien on the vehicle to be additional insured or lender's loss payable. The insurance agent can provide these change on the certificate.

ARTICLES OF INCORPORATION (for corporation) or OF ORGANIZATION (for LLC) - (see appendix for samples)

What is it: It's the "birth certificate" of a business, with basic information of the entity.

Why is it needed: To verify the full legal name of the business (with the exact spelling and punctuation), the type of business (corporation or LLC) the date of inception (there is a classic stamp "Filed on mm/dd/yyyy" on the first page usually which confirms the official creation date of the business, it can be an e-stamp as a bar code showing the date the business filed with the State), the ownership structure (it shows who are the principals of the business), the place of inception (to verify the address is in which State, that matches the current State of operations of the business), the business purpose of the company (what is the business doing).

Also, Articles of Amendment will be required if the business changed its legal name or ownership structure since its creation, so the lender can verify the history of the changes in order and confirm it is always the same entity.

<u>Where to find it</u>: You should have received a hard copy of it from the Secretary of State. Some States make them available for free on their website, download the pdf file. If not, you might have to pay a small fee either to have it as a pdf or mailed/faxed to you.

BY-LAWS (for corporation) **or OPERATING AGREEMENT** (for LLC) **or PARTNERSHIP AGREEMENT** (for partnership)

<u>What is it</u>: These legal documents define the structure and day-to-day roles of the principals of a business. It gives rules and regulations to organize the business' operations and its management. They are not issued by the State, they are written by the business' principals with or without an attorney's help, for internal use only. If they have been modified by minutes, attached them as well to the document.

<u>Why is it needed</u>: It's the legal structure of the entity, the lender needs to know how is organized a business and who is authorized to sign on behalf to the company in case of an unfortunate events like lawsuit, bankruptcy or default on the SBA loan.

<u>Where to find it</u>: You may have written it already and kept it with you or with an attorney, especially if the company has multiple partners. If you have not written the document yet (which is the case for many small family owned businesses or single member business), you can create one from templates online from which you can personalize with your business information and State, or write it with an attorney.

CERTIFICATE OF GOOD STANDING or "ACTIVE STATUS" (for all except sole proprietor)

<u>What is it</u>: A State-issued document that certifies the business exists currently, is in good standing with the State (current on its statutory requirements), therefore authorized to do business in that State. A print out from Internet showing the status of the business is fine as well.

<u>Why is it needed</u>: To verify the business indeed is active and in good standing with the State. If not, the business must contact the Secretary of States to proceed to the late filing and pay filing fee and possible late filing fee. The business is not eligible if the status is suspended by the Franchise Tax Board, or inactive/forfeited or dissolved. It needs to be active/good standing status. Make sure to provide the most recent one, usually one issued within the last 10 days of the application. Some lenders might actually get it for you if it's free to download it online, it's faster and they can check right away basic identification info of the business. It also confirms the legal business name, date of

inception, the name of the principals.

Where to find it: Most of the time viewable online for free on the Secretary of State website, just print out the page or save it as a pdf page. Make sure you print/save with your Internet browser option showing the link of the page and the date of consultation. Provide this certificate for each State where the business is in.

BUSINESS LICENSE (if any)

What is it: Some industries require that a business holds a permit or license to be able to operate. General contractors for example may need a license in some States.

Why is it needed: The lender needs to have it to make sure the business is properly licensed to conduct its activity. Without a mandatory license or permit, the business is illegal and an SBA loan can't be granted.

Where to find it: Within your business files, you may be able to get a copy from the County Clerk or the Secretary of State if you lost it.

DBA or FICTITIOUS BUSINESS NAME STATEMENT (if any)

What is it: DBA stands for "Doing Business As". If a company is doing business under a different name than its legal registered business name, and is not the owner's last name, that company needs to file with the State or County. The statement is a proof the fictitious name has been filed with the required fee under the law of the State in which it operates.

Why is it needed: To verify how many names the business is using and to make sure the fictitious name belongs to the same company.

Where to find it: Within your business files at home, you can ask a copy from the County Clerk or the Secretary of State.

WIRE INSTRUCTION and/or COPY OF VOIDED BUSINESS CHECK

What is it: These are not necessarily both required, one might be enough for the lender. It is simply a check from your business bank account on which you write "void". And the wire instructions indicates the routing number and account number for your business bank account to receive a domestic wire.

<u>Why is it needed</u>: The SBA lender needs to have the business banking account details, to wire the loan funds.

<u>Where to find it</u>: Your business check book, or ask a print out of a check from the teller desk of your local branch. The wiring instructions can be found on most Bank's website or ask your representative at the bank to send you the form.

BUSINESS TRENDS EXPLANATION (see appendix)

<u>What is it</u>: Write some explanation regarding your business trends, look back page 22 Part Two, Chapter One, III. Eligible use of the funds, look for the Tip paragraph.

<u>Why is it needed</u>: This can help speed up your application and shows you know what you are up to.

<u>Where to find it</u>: You can use the template in the appendix on page 90.

II. Location

LEASE (business location leased only)

<u>What is it</u>: The lease signed between your business and a landlord is the contract by which the landlord conveys a property to the lessee (the business) for a specified time in return of a periodic payment.

<u>Why is it needed</u>: The lender checks that the lessee is indeed the business and that the address is the correct business location. If the lease was signed between you (as an individual) and the landlord, you can add the business with an amendment to the lease specifying the lease is being now between the business legal name and the landlord. **The lessee must be the business**.

The lender must verify that the lease is still current and that the lessee has an option to renew the lease for the maturity of the SBA loan. If not, the lender will give you a form to complete with landlord, agreeing both to an OPTION TO RENEW the lease, should it expire and that the SBA loan of 10 years is still outstanding. It doesn't bind the landlord nor the lessee to renew the lease, should one of them want to stop it. It simply gives an option, exercisable during the term of the SBA loan.

The lender will provide you with a form known as LANDLORD SUBORDINATION AGREEMENT, which is not shown in this appendix because each lender can edit their own form. This subordination agreement is required by the SBA. In case of default on your SBA loan, the lender needs to have the landlord consent that he will not block access to the business premises during a certain period (usually 30 days), the time necessary for the lender to recoup any assets as collateral for the loan. They need to make sure the landlord is not going to interfere, so the lender can have priority to seize the assets as quickly as possible to recover the loss on the defaulted loan.

Tip

Start a conversation with your landlord right away if you are serious about applying for an SBA 7(a) loan. It will ease the process of your application when the lender will require you both to sign the subordination agreement.

If you own in your personal name or through another business name the building in which the business applying for the loan is operating, then you need to have a lease between you (or your affiliate business) and your business applying for the SBA loan. There are templates online you can find and set up for your own situation. You will then sign the Landlord subordination and Option to renew as both the landlord and the tenant, since you are leasing to "yourself" (to your business). Make the lease last at least for the term of the SBA loan, (like 10 years) so you don't have to sign an Option to renew.

Where to find it: In your own files, your landlord or his real estate broker will have a copy of it.

PROOF OF HOME OWNERSHIP (home operated business only)

What is it: It can be a grant or title deed, or the most recent real estate property tax bill paid for your home address.

Why is it needed: To confirm the business owner owns the home where his home operated business takes place.

Where to find it: In your files. Some States or County assessors give free access online to property ownership information (name, address, year of acquisition, taxes paid and dues) You can print that page out showing the assessor web-page source and the date of the web-search.

To find your local assessor portal, you can make an internet search with the key words "property tax assessment" plus "name of your county". Make sure the results are for the county of your State. Searches can be make either by name, parcel number, or address.

HOME MORTGAGE LAST STATEMENT (home operated business only)

What is it: The most recent mortgage statement for your home address.

Why is it needed: As the business is home operated, it is required to ensure there is no missed payment on the home mortgage. Being in trouble paying housing payments can jeopardize the business activity.

Where to find it: If lost ask for a copy from your bank branch.

ENVIRONMENTAL QUESTIONNAIRE (business location owned only)

What is it: It is a set of questions from the SBA to assess the level of environmental risk on the business property.

Why is it needed: It is part of the environmental due diligence requirement to search for hazardous contamination of the soil, and avoid potential costs and risk for the business and its SBA lender. This questionnaire is required and the lender will run a Records Search with Risk Assessment. Depending on the business type (gas station) or soil history (used to be underground oil tanks) or proximity of environmentally sensitive industries (dry cleaners), a Phase 1 Environment might be required to pursue with the SBA route. It can cost on average between $1,500 to $5,500 and delay the application for a month. If a Phase 2 is required, consider if it is worth it to continue the SBA route as it will be a considerable delay. A Phase 2 is a physical inspection of the potential environment hazard.

Where to find it: The lender will provide you its form to complete.

COMMERCIAL MORTGAGE LAST STATEMENT (business location owned only)

<u>What is it</u>: The most recent mortgage statement for your commercial mortgage on the business building.

<u>Why is it needed</u>: To verify that the name and address match with the guarantor's information. Make sure there are no late payments or fees.

<u>Where to find it</u>: Either you receive it by mail or available online.

PROOF OF COMMERCIAL PROPERTY OWNERSHIP (business location owned only)

<u>What is it</u>: Same as explained above regarding proof of ownership except this time for a commercial property. It can be a grant or title deed or most recent real estate property tax bill paid for the commercial address.

<u>Why is it needed</u>: To confirm the business owner owns directly or through an affiliate the commercial property where the business operates.

<u>Where to find it</u>: In your files. Some States or County assessors give free access online to property ownership information (name, address, year of acquisition, taxes paid and dues). You can print that page showing the assessor web-page source and the date of the web-search.

III.Insurance

Tip
If you don't have insurance yet, quickly get quotes from www.insureon.com for the coverages you will need, that way you are ready to move fast with your application.

BUSINESS PERSONAL PROPERTY* (see appendix)

<u>What is it</u>: Also known as Evidence of Property Insurance. It is the basic insurance coverage for all the assets that belong to your business (except real estate property). The lender will require a certificate of insurance from the insurance company.

<u>Why is it needed</u>: A business owner you should insure your business assets so in the event they get damaged or stolen you can recover their cost.   The SBA lender will also require insurance for these assets and will require that it be named as an insured.

<u>Where to find it</u>: Your business insurance agent can provide the certificate to you with the specifics requested by the SBA lender regarding endorsements and special mentions.

---

*HOME OWNER'S INSURANCE

If you are a home operated business and your assets total value is less than $5,000 you don't need to purchase a Business Personal Property insurance unless you plan to purchase bigger equipment with the SBA loan. By staying under this asset value limit, you can provide the lender proof of home owner's insurance instead. Ask your agent to edit a certificate for you with the endorsements required by the lender.

GENERAL LIABILITY (see appendix)

<u>What is it</u>: This insurance policy covers businesses for bodily injury, personal injury, and property damage caused by the business' operations, products, or if someone gets injured on the business' premises. The proof of insurance is on a certificate, usually Acord form 25.

<u>Why is it needed</u>: This type of insurance is highly recommended. Injuries and property damage can cause a business bankruptcy. In some cases, you can't work with clients or can't get a lease if you have not this type of insurance. The SBA lender will require proof of insurance.

<u>Where to find it</u>: Your business insurance agent can provide the certificate to you with the specifics requested by the SBA lender regarding endorsements and special mentions. Generally, you will need a policy with $1,000,000 coverage per occurrence, which is not expensive (few hundred dollars to one or two thousand dollars a year).

BUILDING PROPERTY INSURANCE (if building owned)

<u>What is it</u>: It is the insurance policy covering the real estate property where the business operates. The proof of current coverage of the building is usually on an Acord Form 27 or 28.

<u>Why is it needed</u>: The building is collateral to the loan and needs to be insured as well as its contents.

<u>Where to find it</u>: Your business insurance agent can provide the certificate to you with the specifics requested by the SBA lender regarding endorsements and special mentions.

WORKER COMPENSATION (if required by your State)

<u>What is it</u>: It is the insurance policy paid by an employer covering its employees in case they get injured or ill while employed.

<u>Why is it needed</u>: Some States require small business with only one employee to have worker compensation, some will require it starting with 3 or 4 employees. You need to know this for your <u>employee's safety</u>. The lender will verify what the Labor Department of your State requires. The information can be asked to that department, you can also check on your State's Labor Department website, they usually provide guidelines about worker compensation coverage.
This insurance policy provides wages replacement and medical benefits for the injured workers. It concerns employees (that are paid with W2), not sub-contractors. If you hire sub-contractors, in most states you don't have to provide worker compensation for these workers.

<u>Where to find it</u>: The policy is usually renewed every year, you should have been mailed a certificate or notice proving the business is insured during the current year. You can ask your worker compensation insurance provider to send you a proof of current coverage.

MALPRACTICE INSURANCE (for health care professionals and lawyers)

What is it: It is a professional liability insurance usually mandatory for health care professionals and lawyers. This insurance coverage protects health care providers against patients who claim they received negligent or intentionally harmful treatment decisions. It protects lawyers who are sued by their clients claiming they suffered a loss because of the lawyer's mistake or negligence.

Why is it needed: These professions require specific insurance since lawsuits can result in huge dollar amounts paid that a small business owner could never afford himself. Therefore, the SBA lender needs to verify the business holds such coverage.

Where to find it: You may have a notice proof of current coverage in your files, or ask your insurance agent to prepare a certificate providing the details of the coverage according to your profession.

FLOOD INSURANCE (only if located in a flood zone)

It is not on the checklists, because the lender will determine if you are in a flood zone.

What is it: Insurance that covers building and/or contents owned against flood events.

Why is it needed: If your business location is in a flood zone according to flood map of the FEMA (Flood Emergency Management Agency), the SBA lender requires your business to be insured. The SBA lender will do the map search and provide you guidelines.

Where to find it: Your business insurance agent can provide the certificate to you with the specific requests of the SBA lender regarding endorsement and special mentions.

IV.   Guarantors

COLOR PHOTO OF DRIVER LICENSE (front + back)

What is it: Your current driver license.

Why is it needed: To confirm identity of the guarantor. A color copy helps have better visibility and make sure the photo is the same person.

<u>Where to find it</u>: Probably in your wallet!

3 LAST YEARS OF INDIVIDUAL TAX RETURNS

<u>What is it</u>: It is the IRS form 1040.

<u>Why is it needed</u>: The lender verifies the business and the personal financials of its owners to make sure they could repay the loan. It also shows if the household has ownership in other ventures and provides details on real estate owned.

<u>Where to find it</u>: In your own files at home or ask your CPA.

MOST RECENT PAY-STUB OR LAST W2

<u>What is it</u>: The pay slip or pay stub of a periodic statement received by an employee earning a salary showing the breakdown of its pay for that period, usually 2 weeks or 1 month, and the employer's name. The W2 is an IRS form, completed by the employer and sent to both the employee and the IRS at the end of each year to report the annual wages and amount of taxes withheld from the paycheck.

<u>Why is it needed</u>: If the guarantor is earning wages, whether from a part time job (outside of his business applying for the SBA loan) or he is paying himself wages from his business applying for the SBA loan, it is another verification step the lender will want to check. It confirms the source of personal income. If it is extra wages from another job it also gives the proof of this income in the file for the SBA since the financial underwriting will account that income for the guarantor's ability to repay the loan.

<u>Where to find it</u>: In your own files at home.

HOME MORTGAGE LAST STATEMENT

<u>What is it</u>: The most recent statement issued for your home mortgage. If you own several properties, the most recent statement for each mortgage.

<u>Why is it needed</u>: It is required usually when the mortgage has not been reported on the credit report of the guarantor. The lender must verify the monthly housing payment, make sure no late payments exist and that the address and name of the property owner are

correct.

<u>Where to find it</u>: You can download your statement on your online banking usually, or you receive it monthly by mail.

FORM 413 (see appendix)

<u>What is it</u>: Personal financial statement SBA form, to complete by each person guaranteeing the 7(a) loan.

<u>Why is it needed</u>: The lender will require financial information on this form (income, assets, liabilities, etc....) for each guarantor to analyzing their ability to repay the loan.

<u>Where to find it</u>: On the SBA website www.sba.gov/about-sba/sba-performance/policy-regulations/standard-operating-procedures/sba-forms , make sure to use the most updated/current version, attached in the appendix is the current one as of October 2017.

FORM 1919 (see appendix)

<u>What is it</u>: It is an SBA form required for each guarantor on the loan. The purpose of this form is to collect information about the applicant, loan request, indebtedness, information about the principals, information about current or previous government financing, and certain other disclosures.

<u>Why is it needed</u>: To verify the eligibility of the applicant.

<u>Where to find it</u>: On the SBA website www.sba.gov/about-sba/sba-performance/policy-regulations/standard-operating-procedures/sba-forms , make sure to use the most update/current version, attached in the appendix is the current one as of October 2017.

G-845 FORM (for non- US citizen only, see appendix)

<u>What is it</u>: USCIS Form G-845, called the verification request form, is used to confirm the immigration status of someone who wishes to apply for a federal, state, or local license or for any public benefits.

<u>Why is it needed</u>: **Only US citizen or Legal Permanent Resident can apply for an SBA 7(a) loan**. If the applicant is not an American citizen the lender is required to submit this

form to a local SBA district to conduct the verification of his current immigration status.

Where to find it: On the SBA website www.sba.gov/about-sba/sba-performance/policy-regulations/standard-operating-procedures/sba-forms , make sure to use the most update/current version, attached in the appendix is the current one as of October 2017.

RESIDENT ALIEN CARD (for non- US citizen only)

What is it: A color copy of the "green card", the permanent resident card for non- US citizen residing legally and permanently in the United States.

Why is it needed: To verify the legal permanent status of the guarantor, it will be submitted with the G-845 form to the SBA local district.

Where to find it: In your own files or wallet.

CREDIT REPORT EXPLANATION (see appendix)

What is it: An additional document written by you to explain some of your credit report accounts' information like past delinquencies, high revolving balance, recent credit inquiries and public records.

Why is it needed: The lender will analyze with scrutiny the credit report information, it will ask about "negative information" showing. It wants to know if there is pattern of bad credit management that can be an issue in the ability to repay the SBA loan. The explanations must be honest. Being upfront and providing these additional explanations before they are requested will give you a good start in your loan process so you can focus on other parts of your application.

Where to find it: You can write it or I have made a template in the appendix on page 93.

V. Debts to refinance

PROMISSORY NOTE(S)

What is it: A promissory note (or note payable) is a written consent to pay a debt, on demand or on a specified date. The document defines the parties involved and determines the conditions of that agreement.

Why is it needed: The lender who will refinance a business loan, line of credit, or merchant cash advance needs to know the details of these debts to confirm their eligibility to refinance. The promissory note provides names of the creditor, of the debtor, the purpose of the debt, the amount lent, the date it was issued, the terms of the debt, the interest rate, the fees, the balloon payment if any, the collateral secured, the personal guaranty of the business owner and the repayment schedule.

The lender will pay attention to make sure the business name is indeed the debtor and not the owner personally, or another affiliate. It will check that the purpose of the loan is commercial and not for personal expenses. It must make sure the terms of the SBA loan would be better than the debt it refinances. It will point out to you the cost of a balloon payment if any.

Where to find it: In your files, or ask the creditor to provide you a copy of it. Lots of online lenders' customer service can provide it to you within a few hours only and by email. If you deal with a bank, insist you need it immediately, their archive system can be very slow, so don't hesitate to visit the local branch if you have one in your area.

PAYMENT HISTORY LAST 12 MONTHS

What is it: A history of the last 12 months of payments made to refund a certain loan or line of credit or cash advance. Payments can be daily, weekly, monthly, the lender usually requires the last full 12 months.

Why is it needed: To make sure the payments are made in time, in full and there are no delinquencies on a debt about to be refinanced by the SBA lender.

Where to find it: Ask your lender or you might find it online on the lender's online platform, log in and look for payment history or past payments dashboard. Print it out to make sure you have the last 12 months showing.

PAYOFF QUOTE

What is it: It is a statement prepared by the current lender showing the remaining balance on a debt that you are going to pay off soon. The payoff quote shows at a time the remaining due balance, number of payments left and the rate of interest. It also indicates the amount of interest that will be rebated due to prepayment by the borrower. It is a document that can be valid from 1 to 10 days on average.

<u>Why is it needed</u>: When the SBA lender refinances a debt for a business, it repays the full outstanding balance to the current lender directly. Therefore, it needs to know exactly the final amount to wire. The form must include the refinanced lender's wire instruction. The lender can't use your last statement showing the current balance. Payoff quotes provide the final amount a debtor will pay at a time including the interest calculation, and fees for early or third-party prepayment. These numbers change daily or weekly, that's why this quote expires very fast.

<u>Where to find it</u>: Ask the current lender to provide you one, by email is the fastest. Don't be surprised that you might need to ask for a payoff quote update, maybe more than once, as they tend to expire quickly.

12 MONTHS STATEMENTS (for credit cards)

<u>What is it</u>: A credit card monthly statement shows the purchases made with the card every 30 days usually.

<u>Why is it needed</u>: To verify the statements are issued to the business. The cardholder should be the business' name, with authorized user(s) being the business owner or employees for example. The lender will look at the purchases made during the last year, see if they are for general business purpose only. It analyzes the balances at the end of each month to see how the credit limit is used.

<u>Where to find it</u>: They are either mailed to you or available online.

VI. Equipment purchase

INVOICE FOR EQUIPMENT

<u>What is it</u>: It is a price quote or sale invoice handed to you by your merchant for a specific order of equipment you are looking to purchase.

<u>Why is it needed</u>: The lender will purchase the equipment for the business when equipment is itself worth more than $5,000 usually, depends on lender's preferences for collateral. Buying it directly is easier for the bank to take a first lien directly on that equipment as it is identified by its serial number. It is the case especially for big piece of equipment, machinery and vehicles. The invoice can be in the form of an email or a hard

copy letter, with the merchant's name and address, contact details, billing details, the equipment details with price, serial number and date the offer expires if any.

Where to find it: Ask your merchant to prepare it for you.

WIRE INSTRUCTIONS FROM MERCHANT

What is it: The wiring instruction of the merchant to receive the funds from the bank must contain its routing and account numbers.

Why is it needed: To purchase the equipment, the lender will send the funds directly to the merchant's business bank account.

Where to find it: Ask your merchant.

VII. Affiliates

AFFILIATES FORM (see appendix)

What is it: A list of all the ventures in which a guarantor has a percentage of ownership.

Why is it needed: The lender is required to have a certain knowledge on other business(es) owned by the guarantors. It needs to know the name, industry, percentage of ownership, three last years of net receipts and number of employees. If a guarantor owns another business at least 50% or more, he will need to provide the lender with the last three years of tax returns from that other business. The lender needs to know if an affiliate business is doing well financially. If the business owner is struggling with that other business and has a major loss for example, it could be a bad indicator that the SBA loan might be used in fact to help that failing business. The SBA loan can't be used for another business than the one it was granted to, even if they are owned by the same person.

Note: You might hear about "Corporate guaranty" and "co-borrowing business".

First one refers to an affiliate business owned 50% or more by a guarantor, that will be a guarantor of the SBA loan for the benefit of the business taking the loan. Let's say Mr. Joe owns Company A and a second business called Company B. Company A is the one applying for the SBA loan, it is a bakery shop. Company B is an auto accessories shop. Both totally different industries, but owned by Mr. Joe 100%. If the financials of company A and of Mr. Joe together doesn't seem enough to support the monthly payment of the loan, or Mr. Joe's income comes mostly from the Company B, the lender can ask Company B to be a corporate guarantor on the SBA loan, the same way Mr. Joe is a personal guarantor on the loan, in case the Company A fails to repay the loan.

In the second situation, "co borrowing business" refers to an affiliate business owned also by the same guarantor of the applicant business, that is in the same industry and will borrow the funds as well from the SBA loan for its own operations. Therefore, if Company A and Company B are a bakery shop and a coffee shop for example, they are in the same industry and the risk are the funds of the loan will flow between the two entities. The lender therefore makes the two businesses co borrow on the loan. Therefore, all documentation asked for one business will have to be provided also for the affiliate business.

Where to find it: In the appendix of this book is a template on page 89.

Chapter Four

Tips during the loan process

At this point, you should be ready to apply! You can find a list of the top 100 most active SBA7(a) lenders[6] on the official SBA website https://www.sba.gov/lenders-top-100 . Let's recap below the steps and tips to successfully package your application, submit it to the lenders and be on top of it during the loan process.

1. Make sure to **maintain your credit score as high as possible** during the full loan process.

2. If you have late payments or public records on your credit report, prepare explanations, you can use the "credit report explanation" template on page 93.

3. Check that you have no active IRS tax lien. If you have taxes due, prepare a copy of your installment agreement.

4. List all your business debts in the template in the appendix on page 91.

5. List all your business' assets in the template in the appendix on page 90.

6. Be prepared to explain your business trends, you can use the template I made in the appendix on page 92

7. Review the checklists on pages 60 to 62 to have all your documents handy. Stay organized and have copies ready.

8. If you lease your business location, talk to the landlord about the subordination agreement as described on pages 69-70.

9. **Always be responsive to bank's questions**, the same day or the next one.

---

[6] See link below to look for the "Top 100 Most Active SBA 7(a) Lenders" : https://www.sba.gov/lenders-top-100

10. Be accurate and forthcoming in your answers.

11. **Keep your documents up to date during the loan process**.

12. Maintain constant contact with the lender, ask him which documents are still missing and what is the next step.

13. Set a time every day to work on your application and communicate with the lender. **Don't procrastinate!**

"YOU CAN DO IT!"

In conclusion, an SBA 7(a) loan is not as hard to get as many might think as long the business and its owners are eligible. Getting the paperwork done should be a matter of a few days if the records are organized.

An SBA loan can save tons of interest and fees but does require a bit of documentation. If you are not in a rush to get the money the next day and have a bit of patience, you won't regret it.

Take the time to analyze what your business' needs are and build your plan. The smartest way to obtain funding for your plan is to be prepared and organized. This book is exactly what you need to prepare your SBA loan application.

When you are ready to apply, just follow the easy steps and tips in this book! I wish you the best for your business. It was my pleasure to help you!

"If you liked this guide, please leave a review online, thank you!"
Claire

Index

Appendix

Affiliates Form

AFFILIATES FORM

Business Name	% of ownership	Industry	Last 3 years of Net Revenue	# of employees
Example: Company B	John Smith who owns 100% of Company A applying for the SBA loan, also owns 100% of Company B.	Food retail	2014: $25,000 2015: $35,000 2016: $43,000	3

Business Name	% of ownership	Industry	Last 3 years of Net Revenue	# of employees

Assets List

BUSINESS ASSETS LIST

Quantity	Asset	Brand/Model	Year Acquired	Serial Number or ID Number or VIN Number for asset worth $5,000 each	Original Value (when purchased)	Market Value (as of today)	Current lien holder (Y/N)	If lien holder, name of lender	Outstanding balance with lien holder
Example: 4	Desk and Chairs	Multiple	2010	n/a	$700	$250	N		
Example: 2	Computers	HP	2013	n/a	$2000	$500	N		
Example: 1	Truck	Ford	2015	Vin number ###	$15,000	$11000	Y	Bank One	$9,000

Quantity	Asset	Brand/Model	Year Acquired	Serial Number or ID Number or VIN Number for asset worth $5,000 each	Original Value (when purchased)	Market Value (as of today)	Current lien holder (Y/N)	If lien holder, name of lender	Outstanding balance with lien holder

Business Debt Schedule

BUSINESS DEBTS SCHEDULE

Name of lender	Type of debt (credit card, line of credit, term loan, cash advance...)	Origination date (year, month if known)	Outstanding balance	Minimum monthly payment	Months remaining (if any)	Refinanced by the SBA Loan? Y/N
Example: Lender A	Term Loan	October 2009	$35,860	$427	84	N
Example: Lender B	Credit card	May 2012	$8,300	$250	n/a	N
Example: Lender C	Cash advance	June 2016	$12,000	$1,000	12	Y

Name of lender	Type of debt (credit card, line of credit, term loan, cash advance...)	Origination date (year, month if known)	Outstanding balance	Minimum monthly payment	Months remaining (if any)	Refinanced by the SBA Loan? Y/N

BUSINESS TRENDS EXPLANATION

Explain the trends big dollar changes in profit, expenses or revenues, for the past two or three years. Write about five sentences per answer, the more the better. Use as many pages as needed.

Tip
Think about what decisions, actions, strategies and events, may have impacted the revenue/expenses (example: if you changed product line, suppliers, improved marketing, hired more staff, expensed more in some items, acquired new clients…) It has to be related to the business, your industry, your local area, so the lender understands what happened.

Trend for year #1	
Trend for year #2	
Trend for year #3	
Trend for interim period and how the loan proceeds will help the business growth.	

CREDIT REPORT EXPLANATION

Inquiries since last 3 months	For each inquiry, briefly explain what it was for and if you opened or are in process of opening new debt.
Late payments for last 12 months	For each debt with at least one late payment, briefly explain why the delinquency happened.
High- revolving balance	Explain why you hold a high balance on your credit cards and what is your plan to pay it down to zero.
Public records	If you have had past bankruptcy/tax lien/ judgement released or other public records on your credit report, explain in detail what happened, what actions you took to solve the issues and how the situation is now different from the past to avoid it from happening again.

Form 1919 (1/6)

OMB Control No.: 3245-0348
Expiration Date: 04/17/2017

BORROWER INFORMATION FORM
For use with all 7(a) Programs

The purpose of this form is to collect identifying information about the applicant, loan request, indebtedness, information about the principals, information about current or previous government financing, and certain other disclosures. The information also facilitates background checks as authorized by Section 7(a)(1)(B) of the Small Business Act, 15 U.S.C. 636(a)(1)(B). This form is to be completed by the Small Business Applicant and submitted to an SBA Participating Lender.

To be completed by the following:
(With the exception of guarantors, all parties listed below are considered "Associates" of the small business applicant.)

- For a sole proprietorship, the sole proprietor;
- For a partnership, all general partners and all limited partners owning 20% or more of the equity of the firm;
- For a corporation, all owners of 20% or more of the corporation and each officer and director;
- For limited liability companies (LLCs), all members owning 20% or more of the company, each officer, director, and managing member;
- Any person hired by the business to manage day-to-day operations; and
- Any other person who is guaranteeing the loan, if required by SBA.

For clarification regarding any of the questions, you should contact the SBA Participating Lender that will be processing the loan request.

NAME OF BUSINESS APPLYING FOR LOAN ("APPLICANT"): _____

YOUR NAME: _____ TITLE: _____

SOCIAL SECURITY NUMBER: _____ DATE OF BIRTH: _____

PLACE OF BIRTH (City & State or Foreign Country): _____

Veteran**	1=Non-Veteran; 2=Veteran-Other; 3=Service-Disabled Veteran; 4=Not Disclosed.					
Gender**	M=Male; F=Female; N=Not Disclosed					
Race**	1=American Indian or Alaska Native; 2=Asian; 3=Black or African-American; 4=Native Hawaiian or Pacific Islander; 5=White; X=Not Disclosed					
Ethnicity**	H=Hispanic or Latino; N=Not Hispanic or Latino; Y=Not Disclosed					
Owner	% Owned	Veteran	Gender	Race	Ethnicity	List proprietors, partners, officers, directors, all holders of outstanding stock. 100% of ownership must be shown. Use separate sheet if necessary. Please reference the above codes to complete this table for each owner of the applicant business. More than one race may be selected.

** The gender/race/ethnicity/veteran data is collected for program reporting purposes only. Disclosure is voluntary and has no bearing on the credit decision.

ALL QUESTIONS MUST BE ANSWERED AND ARE SUBJECT TO VERIFICATION BY SBA
(1) Are you presently subject to an indictment, criminal information, arraignment, or other means by which formal criminal charges are brought in any jurisdiction?..Yes ☐ ... No ☐
(2) Have you been arrested in the past six months for any criminal offense? ....Yes ☐ ... No ☐
(3) For any criminal offense – other than a minor vehicle violation – have you ever: 1) been convicted; 2) plead guilty; 3) plead nolo contendere; 4) been placed on pretrial diversion; or 5) been placed on any form of parole or probation (including probation before judgment)? ....Yes ☐ ... No ☐
(4) Has an application for the loan you are applying for now ever been submitted to SBA or to a
    Certified Development Company or lender in connection with any SBA program?....................Yes ☐ .....No ☐

Form 1919 (2/6)

(5) Are you presently debarred, suspended, proposed for debarment, declared ineligible, or
voluntarily excluded from participation in this transaction by any Federal department or agency?Yes ☐ ...No ☐

(6) If you are at least a 50% or more owner of the applicant business, are you more than 60 days
delinquent on any obligation to pay child support arising under an administrative order, court
order, repayment agreement between the holder and a custodial parent, or repayment agreement
between the holder and a state agency providing child support enforcement services? ....Yes ☐...No ☐

**If "YES" to Question 1, the loan request is ineligible for SBA assistance. If there is a "YES" response to
Question 2 or 3, you must complete SBA Form 912 and furnish details on a separate sheet, including dates,
location, fines, sentences, whether misdemeanor or felony, dates of parole/probation, unpaid fines or penalties,
name(s) under which charged, and any other pertinent information. If "YES" to Questions 2 or 3, the lender
will be required to conduct a background check and make a character determination in accordance with the
procedures described in SOP 50 10 5. If "YES" to Question 3 and you are currently on parole or probation
(including probation before judgment), the loan request is ineligible for SBA assistance. If the charge resulting
in a "YES" was a single misdemeanor that was subsequently dropped without prosecution, you must provide
documentation from the appropriate court or prosecutor's office along with the completed Form 912.**

**If "YES" to Questions 4, 5 or 6, this application may not be submitted to SBA under any delegated or
expedited processing method, but must be submitted to the Standard 7(a) Loan Guaranty Processing Center
(LGPC) for non-delegated processing. The only exception is an application that was declined under a 7(a)
Small Loan due to the applicant's credit score may be submitted under SBA Express procedures. Note: This
does not mean that your loan will be denied, only that your lender will need to use different SBA procedures
to process the loan.**

(7) Are you a U.S. Citizen?...Yes ☐....No ☐
If "No," are you a Lawful Permanent resident alien?...Yes ☐....No ☐
Provide Alien Registration Number _____

(8) Are any of your business' products or services exported or do you plan to begin exporting as a
result of this loan?..Yes ☐...No ☐
If ""Yes," provide the estimated total export sales this loan will support: $_____

(9) Is your business a franchise? ....Yes ☐...No ☐

(10) Does the Applicant business have any Affiliates? ....Yes ☐...No ☐

Affiliation exists when one individual or entity controls or has the power to control another or when a third
party or parties control or have the power to control both. SBA considers factors such as ownership,
management previous relationships with or ties to another entity, and contractual relationships when
determining whether affiliation exists. The complete definition of affiliation is found at 13 CFR 121.103. (See
also, 13 CFR 121.107 and 121.301.) An "Affiliate" includes, for example: (1) a parent company; (2)
subsidiaries and other companies that are owned or controlled by the Applicant; (3) companies in which an
officer, director, general partner, managing member or party owning 20% or more is also an officer, director,
general partner, managing member or 20% or greater owner of the Applicant; (4) companies or individuals with
unexercised options to own 50% or more of the Applicant's stock; and (5) companies that have entered into
agreements to merge with the Applicant.
If answered "yes," attach a listing of all Affiliates to this form.

(11) Have you, the Applicant, its Affiliates, or any business owned or controlled by you or any
Associate ever obtained a direct or guaranteed loan from SBA or any other Federal agency or
been a guarantor on such a loan? (This includes student loans and disaster loans.) .... Yes ☐...No ☐
(a) If you answered "Yes" to Question 11, is any of the financing currently delinquent?...........Yes ☐...No ☐
(b) If you answered "Yes" to Question 11, did any of this financing ever default and cause a
loss to the Government? .... Yes ☐...No ☐

(12) What is the existing number of employees currently employed by the business? _____

(13) Number of jobs to be created as a result of the loan? _____ Number of jobs that will be retained as a
result of the loan that would have been lost otherwise?_____

(14) Have you or the Applicant used (or intend to use) a packager, broker, accountant, lawyer, etc.to assist
in (a) preparing the loan application or any related materials and/or (b) referring the loan to the
lender?..Yes ☐...No ☐
If answer is "Yes," a SBA Form 159 7(a) will need to be completed by the Applicant and the lender.

Form 1919 (3/6)

(15) Will more than $10,000 of the loan proceeds be used for construction? ....Yes ☐...No ☐
  If answer is "Yes," a SBA Form 601 will need to be completed.

(16) Are any of the Applicant's revenues derived from gambling or from the sale of products or services, or the presentation of any depiction, displays or live performances, of a prurient sexual nature? ....Yes ☐...No ☐

(17) Is the loan request for a Community Advantage Pilot Program loan?　　　　　　　　　　　Yes ☐...No ☐
  If answer is "Yes," a SBA Form 2449, Community Advantage Addendum will need to be completed.

SBA may not provide financial assistance to an applicant where there is any appearance of a conflict of interest with an SBA or other governmental employee. If any of the questions below are answered "False", this application may not be submitted under any delegated or expedited processing method, but must be submitted to the LGPC for non-delegated processing. Note: This does not mean that your loan will be denied, only that your lender will need to use different SBA procedures to process the loan.

(18) No SBA employee, or the household member (see definition at * below) of an SBA employee, is a sole proprietor, partner, officer, director, or stockholder with a 10 percent or more interest, of the Applicant. [13 CFR 105.204]　　　　　　　　　　　　　　　　　　　　　　　　True____ False_____

(19) No former SBA employee, who has been separated from SBA for less than one year prior to the request for financial assistance, is an employee, owner, partner, attorney, agent, owner of stock, officer, director, creditor or debtor of the Applicant. [13 CFR 105.203]　　　　　　　　　　　True____ False_____

(20) No member of Congress, or an appointed official or employee of the legislative or judicial branch of the Federal Government, is a sole proprietor, general partner, officer, director, or stockholder with a 10 percent or more interest, or household member of such individual, of the Applicant.
  [13 CFR 105.301(c)]　　　　　　　　　　　　　　　　　　　　　　　True____ False_____

(21) No Government employee having a grade of at least GS-13 or higher is a sole proprietor, general partner, officer, director, or stockholder with a 10 percent or more interest, or a household member of such individual, of the Applicant. [13 CFR 105.301(a)]　　　　　　　　　　　True____ False_____

(22) No member or employee of a Small Business Advisory Council or a SCORE volunteer is a sole proprietor, general partner, officer, director, or stockholder with a 10 percent or more interest, or a household member of such individual, of the Applicant. [13 CFR 105.302(a)]　　　　True____ False_____

* A "**household member**" of an SBA employee includes: a) the spouse of the SBA employee; b) the minor children of said individual; and c) the blood relatives of the employee, and the blood relatives of the employee's spouse who reside in the same place of abode as the employee.[13 CFR 105.201(d)]

Form 1919 (4/6)

Please read the following restrictions regarding use of federal financial assistance programs. If you understand them fully and agree to them, sign your name at the end of this document.

SBA is required to withhold or limit financial assistance, to impose special conditions on approved loans, to provide special notices to applicants or borrowers and to require special reports and data from borrowers in order to comply with legislation passed by the Congress and Executive Orders issued by the President and by the provisions of various inter-agency agreements. SBA has issued regulations and procedures that implement these laws and executive orders. These are contained in Parts 112, 113, and 117 of Title 13 of the Code of Federal Regulations and in Standard Operating Procedures.

Privacy Act (5 U.S.C. 552a) -- Any person can request to see or get copies of any personal information that SBA has in his or her file when that file is retrieved by individual identifiers such as name or social security numbers. Requests for information about another party may be denied unless SBA has the written permission of the individual to release the information to the requestor or unless the information is subject to disclosure under the Freedom of Information Act.

Under the provisions of the Privacy Act, you are not required to provide your social security number. Failure to provide your social security number may not affect any right, benefit or privilege to which you are entitled. Disclosures of name and other personal identifiers are, however, required for a benefit, as SBA requires an individual seeking assistance from SBA to provide it with sufficient information for it to make a character determination. In determining whether an individual is of good character, SBA considers the person's integrity, candor, and disposition toward criminal actions. Additionally, SBA is specifically authorized to verify your criminal history, or lack thereof, pursuant to section 7(a)(1)(B), 15 USC Section 636(a)(1)(B) of the Small Business Act (the Act). Further, for all forms of assistance, SBA is authorized to make all investigations necessary to ensure that a person has not engaged in acts that violate or will violate the Act or the Small Business Investment Act, 15 USC Sections 634(b)(11) and 687(b)(a), respectively. For these purposes, you are asked to voluntarily provide your social security number to assist SBA in making a character determination and to distinguish you from other individuals with the same or similar name or other personal identifier.

The Privacy Act authorizes SBA to make certain "routine uses" of information protected by that Act. One such routine use is the disclosure of information maintained in SBA's investigative files system of records when this information indicates a violation or potential violation of law, whether civil, criminal, or administrative in nature. Specifically, SBA may refer the information to the appropriate agency, whether Federal, State, local or foreign, charged with responsibility for, or otherwise involved in investigation, prosecution, enforcement or prevention of such violations. Another routine use is disclosure to other Federal agencies conducting background checks; only to the extent the information is relevant to the requesting agencies' function. See, 74 F.R. 14890 (2009), and as amended from time to time for additional background and other routine uses.

Right to Financial Privacy Act of 1978 (12 U.S.C. 3401) -- This is notice to you as required by the Right to Financial Privacy Act of 1978, of SBA's access rights to financial records held by financial institutions that are or have been doing business with you or your business, including any financial institutions participating in a loan or loan guaranty. The law provides that SBA shall have a right of access to your financial records in connection with its consideration or administration of assistance to you in the form of a Government guaranteed loan. SBA is required to provide a certificate of its compliance with the Act to a financial institution in connection with its first request for access to your financial records, after which no further certification is required for subsequent accesses. The law also provides that SBA's access rights continue for the term of any approved loan guaranty agreement. No further notice to you of SBA's access rights is required during the term of any such agreement. The law also authorizes SBA to transfer to another Government authority any financial records included in an application for a loan, or concerning an approved loan or loan guarantee, as necessary to process, service or foreclose on a loan guaranty or collect on a defaulted loan guaranty.

Freedom of Information Act (5 U.S.C. 552) -- This law provides, with some exceptions, that SBA must supply information reflected in agency files and records to a person requesting it. Information about approved loans that will be automatically released includes, among other things, statistics on our loan programs (individual borrowers are not identified in the statistics) and other information such as the names of the borrowers (and their officers, directors, stockholders or partners), the collateral pledged to secure the loan, the amount of the loan, its purpose in general terms and the maturity. Proprietary data on a borrower would not routinely be made available to third parties. All requests under this Act are to be addressed to the nearest SBA office and be identified as a Freedom of Information request.

Flood Disaster Protection Act (42 U.S.C. 4011) -- Regulations have been issued by the Federal Insurance Administration (FIA) and by SBA implementing this Act and its amendments. These regulations prohibit SBA from making certain loans in an FIA designated floodplain unless Federal Flood insurance is purchased as a condition of the loan. Failure to maintain the required level of flood insurance makes the applicant ineligible for any financial assistance from SBA, including disaster assistance.

Form 1919 (5/6)

Executive Orders -- Floodplain Management and Wetland Protection (42 F.R. 26951 and 42 F.R. 26961) -- SBA discourages settlement in or development of a floodplain or a wetland. This statement is to notify all SBA loan applicants that such actions are hazardous to both life and property and should be avoided. The additional cost of flood preventive construction must be considered in addition to the possible loss of all assets and investments due to a future flood.

Occupational Safety and Health Act (15 U.S.C. 651 et seq.) -- This legislation authorizes the Occupational Safety and Health Administration in the Department of Labor to require businesses to modify facilities and procedures to protect employees or pay penalty fees. Businesses can be forced to cease operations or be prevented from starting operations in a new facility. Therefore, SBA may require additional information from an applicant to determine whether the business will be in compliance with OSHA regulations and allowed to operate its facility after the loan is approved and disbursed. Signing this form as an applicant is certification that the OSHA requirements that apply to the applicant business have been determined and that the applicant, to the best of its knowledge, is in compliance. Furthermore, applicant certifies that it will remain in compliance during the life of the loan.

Civil Rights Legislation (13 C.F.R. 112, 113, 117) -- All businesses receiving SBA financial assistance must agree not to discriminate in any business practice, including employment practices and services to the public on the basis of categories cited in 13 C.F.R., Parts 112, 113, and 117 of SBA Regulations. This includes making their goods and services available to handicapped clients or customers. All business borrowers will be required to display the "Equal Employment Opportunity Poster" prescribed by SBA.

Equal Credit Opportunity Act (15 U.S.C. 1691) -- The Federal Equal Credit Opportunity Act prohibits creditors from discriminating against credit applicants on the basis of race, color, religion, national origin, sex, marital status or age (provided the applicant has the capacity to enter into a binding contract); because all or part of the applicant's income derives from any public assistance program, or because the applicant has in good faith exercised any right under the Consumer Credit Protection Act.

Executive Order 11738 -- Environmental Protection (38 F.R. 251621) -- The Executive Order charges SBA with administering its loan programs in a manner that will result in effective enforcement of the Clean Air Act, the Federal Water Pollution Act and other environment protection legislation.

Debt Collection Act of 1982, Deficit Reduction Act of 1984 (31 U.S.C. 3701 et seq. and other titles) -- These laws require SBA to collect aggressively any loan payments which become delinquent. SBA must obtain your taxpayer identification number when you apply for a loan. If you receive a loan, and do not make payments as they come due, SBA may take one or more of the following actions: (1) report the status of your loan(s) to credit bureaus, (2) hire a collection agency to collect your loan, (3) offset your income tax refund or other amounts due to you from the Federal Government, (4) suspend or debar you or your company from doing business with the Federal Government, (5) refer your loan to the Department of Justice or other attorneys for litigation, or (6) foreclose on collateral or take other action permitted in the loan instruments.

Immigration Reform and Control Act of 1986 (Pub. L. 99-603) -- If you are an alien who was in this country illegally since before January 1, 1982, you may have been granted lawful temporary resident status by the United States Immigration and Naturalization Service pursuant to the Immigration Reform and Control Act of 1986. For five years from the date you are granted such status, you are not eligible for financial assistance from the SBA in the form of a loan guaranty under Section 7(a) of the Small Business Act unless you are disabled or a Cuban or Haitian entrant. When you sign this document, you are making the certification that the Immigration Reform and Control Act of 1986 does not apply to you, or if it does apply, more than five years have elapsed since you have been granted lawful temporary resident status pursuant to such 1986 legislation.

Lead-Based Paint Poisoning Prevention Act (42 U.S.C. 4821 et seq.)
Borrowers using SBA funds for the construction or rehabilitation of a residential structure are prohibited from using lead-based paint (as defined in SBA regulations) on all interior surfaces, whether accessible or not, and exterior surfaces, such as stairs, decks, porches, railings, windows and doors, which are readily accessible to children under 7 years of age. A "residential structure" is any home, apartment, hotel, motel, orphanage, boarding school, dormitory, day care center, extended care facility, college or other school housing, hospital, group practice or community facility and all other residential or institutional structures where persons reside.

Executive Order 12549, Debarment and Suspension (13 C.F.R. 145) -- The prospective lower tier participant certifies, by submission of this loan application, that neither it nor its principals are presently debarred, suspended, proposed for debarment, declared ineligible, or voluntarily excluded from participation in this transaction by any Federal department or agency. Where the prospective lower tier participant is unable to certify to any of the statements in this certification, such prospective participants shall attach an explanation to the loan application.

Form 1919 (6/6)

By Signing Below, You Make the Following Representations, Authorizations and Certifications

REPRESENTATIONS AND AUTHORIZATIONS: I represent that I have read the items above and I understand them. I represent that I will comply, whenever applicable, with the hazard insurance, lead-based paint, civil rights or other limitations in this notice. I further represent that all SBA loan proceeds will be used only for business related purposes as specified in the loan application and, to the extent feasible, to purchase only American-made equipment and products. I authorize the SBA Office of Inspector General to request criminal record information about me from criminal justice agencies for the purpose of determining my eligibility for programs authorized by the Small Business Act, as amended.

CERTIFICATION AS TO ACCURACY: I certify that the information provided in this application and the information that I have provided in all supporting documents and forms is true and accurate. I realize that the penalty for knowingly making a false statement to obtain a guaranteed loan from SBA is that I may be fined up to $250,000 and/or be put in jail for up to 5 years under 18 USC § 1001 and if false statements are submitted to a Federally insured institution, I may be fined up to $1,000,000 and/or be put in jail for up to 30 years under 18 USC § 1014.

_____   _____
Signature   Date

_____
Print Name

Form 413 (1/5)

OMB APPROVAL NO.: 3245-0188
EXPIRATION DATE: 01/31/2018

PERSONAL FINANCIAL STATEMENT
7(a) / 504 LOANS AND SURETY BONDS

U.S. SMALL BUSINESS ADMINISTRATION   As of _____, _____

SBA uses the information required by this Form 413 as one of a number of data sources in analyzing the repayment ability and creditworthiness of an application for an SBA guaranteed 7(a) or 504 loan or a guaranteed surety.

Complete this form for: (1) each proprietor; (2) general partner; (3) managing member of a limited liability company (LLC); (4) each owner of 20% or more of the equity of the Applicant (including the assets of the owner's spouse and any minor children); and (5) any person providing a guaranty on the loan

Return completed form to:
For 7(a) loans: the lender processing the application for SBA guaranty
For 504 loans: the Certified Development Company (CDC) processing the application for SBA guaranty
For Surety Bonds: the Surety Company or Agent processing the application for surety bond guaranty

Name	Business Phone
Home Address	Home Phone
City, State, & Zip Code	
Business Name of Applicant	

ASSETS	(Omit Cents)	LIABILITIES	(Omit Cents)
Cash on Hand & in banks...........................$ _____		Accounts Payable................................$ _____	
Savings Accounts....................................$ _____		Notes Payable to Banks and Others..........$ _____	
IRA or Other Retirement Account..................$ _____		(Describe in Section 2)	
(Describe in Section 5)		Installment Account (Auto).....................$ _____	
Accounts & Notes Receivable.....................$ _____		Mo. Payments $ _____	
(Describe in Section 5)		Installment Account (Other)....................$ _____	
Life Insurance – Cash Surrender Value Only......$ _____		Mo. Payments $ _____	
(Describe in Section 8)		Loan(s) Against Life Insurance.................$ _____	
Stocks and Bonds...................................$ _____		Mortgages on Real Estate......................$ _____	
(Describe in Section 3)		(Describe in Section 4)	
Real Estate..$ _____		Unpaid Taxes....................................$ _____	
(Describe in Section 4)		(Describe in Section 6)	
Automobiles..$ _____		Other Liabilities.................................$ _____	
(Describe in Section 5, and include		(Describe in Section 7)	
Year/Make/Model)		Total Liabilities...................................$ 0	
Other Personal Property............................$ _____		Net Worth..$ 0	
(Describe in Section 5)			
Other Assets...$ _____		**Total Liabilities & Net Worth $ 0**	
(Describe in Section 5)		***Must equal total in assets column.**	
Total Assets $ 0			

Section 1. Source of Income.		Contingent Liabilities	
Salary...$ _____		As Endorser or Co-Maker.........................$ _____	
Net Investment Income...............................$ _____		Legal Claims & Judgments.......................$ _____	
Real Estate Income...................................$ _____		Provision for Federal Income Tax...............$ _____	
Other Income (Describe below)*....................$ _____		Other Special Debt................................$ _____	

Description of Other Income in Section 1.

*Alimony or child support payments should not be disclosed in "Other Income" unless it is desired to have such payments counted toward total income.

Form 413 (2/5)

Section 2. Notes Payable to Banks and Others. (Use attachments if necessary. Each attachment must be identified as part of this statement and signed.)

Names and Addresses of Noteholder(s)	Original Balance	Current Balance	Payment Amount	Frequency (monthly, etc.)	How Secured or Endorsed Type of Collateral

Section 3. Stocks and Bonds. (Use attachments if necessary. Each attachment must be identified as part of this statement and signed.)

Number of Shares	Name of Securities	Cost	Market Value Quotation/Exchange	Date of Quotation/Exchange	Total Value

Section 4. Real Estate Owned. (List each parcel separately. Use attachment if necessary. Each attachment must be identified as a part of this statement and signed.)

	Property A	Property B	Property C
Type of Real Estate (e.g. Primary Residence, Other Residence, Rental Property, Land, etc.)			
Address			
Date Purchased			
Original Cost			
Present Market Value			
Name & Address of Mortgage Holder			
Mortgage Account Number			
Mortgage Balance			
Amount of Payment per Month/Year			
Status of Mortgage			

Section 5. Other Personal Property and Other Assets. (Describe, and, if any is pledged as security, state name and address of lien holder, amount of lien, terms of payment and, if delinquent, describe delinquency.)

Section 6. Unpaid Taxes. (Describe in detail as to type, to whom payable, when due, amount, and to what property, if any, a tax lien attaches.)

Section 7. Other Liabilities. (Describe in detail.)

SBA Form 413 (7a/504/SBG) (09-14) **Previous Editions Obsolete**   **Page 2**

Section 8. Life Insurance Held. (Give face amount and cash surrender value of policies – name of insurance company and Beneficiaries.)

I authorize the SBA/Lender/Surety Company to make inquiries as necessary to verify the accuracy of the statements made and to determine my creditworthiness.

CERTIFICATION: (to be completed by each person submitting the information requested on this form)

By signing this form, I certify under penalty of criminal prosecution that all information on this form and any additional supporting information submitted with this form is true and complete to the best of my knowledge. I understand that SBA or its participating Lenders or Certified Development Companies or Surety Companies will rely on this information when making decisions regarding an application for a loan or a surety bond. I further certify that I have read the attached statements required by law and executive order.

Signature _____   Date _____

Print Name _____   Social Security No. _____

Signature _____   Date _____

Print Name _____   Social Security No. _____

NOTICE TO LOAN AND SURETY BOND APPLICANTS: CRIMINAL PENALITIES AND ADMINISTRATIVE REMEDIES FOR FALSE STATEMENTS:

Knowingly making a false statement on this form is a violation of Federal law and could result in criminal prosecution, significant civil penalties, and a denial of your loan or surety bond application. A false statement is punishable under 18 U.S.C. §§ 1001 and 3571 by imprisonment of not more than five years and/or a fine of up to $250,000; under 15 U.S.C. § 645 by imprisonment of not more than two years and/or a fine of not more than $5,000; and, if submitted to a Federally-insured institution, a false statement is punishable under 18 U.S.C. § 1014 by imprisonment of not more than thirty years and/or a fine of not more than $1,000,000. Additionally, false statements can lead to treble damages and civil penalties under the False Claims Act, 31 U.S.C. § 3729, and other administrative remedies including suspension and debarment.

PLEASE NOTE: The estimated average burden hours for the completion of this form is 1.5 hours per response. If you have questions or comments concerning this estimate or any other aspect of this information, please contact Chief, Administrative Branch, U.S. Small Business Administration, Washington, D.C. 20416, and Clearance officer, paper Reduction Project (3245-0188), Office of Management and Budget, Washington, D.C. 20503. PLEASE DO NOT SEND FORMS TO OMB.

PLEASE READ, DETACH, AND RETAIN FOR YOUR RECORDS
STATEMENTS REQUIRED BY LAW AND EXECUTIVE ORDER

SBA is required to withhold or limit financial assistance, to impose special conditions on approved loans, to provide special notices to applicants or borrowers and to require special reports and data from borrowers in order to comply with legislation passed by the Congress and Executive Orders issued by the President and by the provisions of various inter-agency agreements. SBA has issued regulations and procedures that implement these laws and executive orders. These are contained in Parts 112, 113, and 117 of Title 13 of the Code of Federal Regulations and in Standard Operating Procedures.

Privacy Act (5 U.S.C. 552a)
Any person can request to see or get copies of any personal information that SBA has in his or her file when that file is retrieved by individual identifiers such as name or social security numbers. Requests for information about another party may be denied unless SBA has the written permission of the individual to release the information to the requestor or unless the information is subject to disclosure under the Freedom of Information Act.

Under the provisions of the Privacy Act, you are not required to provide your social security number. Failure to provide your social security number may not affect any right, benefit or privilege to which you are entitled. Disclosures of name and other personal identifiers are, however, required for a benefit, as SBA requires an individual seeking assistance from SBA to provide it with sufficient information for it to make a character determination. In determining whether an individual is of good character, SBA considers the person's integrity, candor, and disposition toward criminal actions. Additionally, SBA is specifically authorized to verify your criminal history, or lack thereof, pursuant to section 7(a)(1)(B), 15 USC Section 636(a)(1)(B) of the Small Business Act (the Act). Further, for all forms of assistance, SBA is authorized to make all investigations necessary to ensure that a person has not engaged in acts that violate or will violate the Act or the Small Business Investment Act, 15 USC Sections 634(b)(11) and 687(b)(a), respectively. For these purposes, you are asked to voluntarily provide your social security number to assist SBA in making a character determination and to distinguish you from other individuals with the same or similar name or other personal identifier.

The Privacy Act authorizes SBA to make certain "routine uses" of information protected by that Act. One such routine use is the disclosure of information maintained in SBA's investigative files system of records when this information indicates a violation or potential violation of law, whether civil, criminal, or administrative in nature. Specifically, SBA may refer the information to the appropriate agency, whether Federal, State, local or foreign, charged with responsibility for, or otherwise involved in investigation, prosecution, enforcement or prevention of such violations. Another routine use is disclosure to other Federal agencies conducting background checks; only to the extent the information is relevant to the requesting agencies' function. See, 74 F.R. 14890 (2009), and as amended from time to time for additional background and other routine uses.

Right to Financial Privacy Act of 1978 (12 U.S.C. 3401) -- This is notice to you as required by the Right to Financial Privacy Act of 1978, of SBA's access rights to financial records held by financial institutions that are or have been doing business with you or your business, including any financial institutions participating in a loan or loan guaranty. The law provides that SBA shall have a right of access to your financial records in connection with its consideration or administration of assistance to you in the form of a Government guaranteed loan. SBA is required to provide a certificate of its compliance with the Act to a financial institution in connection with its first request for access to your financial records, after which no further certification is required for subsequent accesses. The law also provides that SBA's access rights continue for the term of any approved loan guaranty agreement. No further notice to you of SBA's access rights is required during the term of any such agreement. The law also authorizes SBA to transfer to another Government authority any financial records included in a application for a loan, or concerning an approved loan or loan guarantee, as necessary to process, service or foreclose on a loan guaranty or collect on a defaulted loan guaranty.

Freedom of Information Act (5 U.S.C. 552)
This law provides, with some exceptions, that SBA must supply information reflected in agency files and records to a person requesting it. Information about approved loans that will be automatically released includes, among other things, statistics on our loan programs (individual borrowers are not identified in the statistics) and other information such as the names of the borrowers (and their officers, directors, stockholders or partners), the collateral pledged to secure the loan, the amount of the loan, its purpose in general terms and the maturity. Proprietary data on a borrower would not routinely be made available to third parties. All requests under this Act are to be addressed to the nearest SBA office and be identified as a Freedom of Information request.

Flood Disaster Protection Act (42 U.S.C. 4011) -- Regulations have been issued by the Federal Insurance Administration (FIA) and by SBA implementing this Act and its amendments. These regulations prohibit SBA from making certain loans in an FIA designated floodplain unless Federal Flood insurance is purchased as a condition of the loan. Failure to maintain the required level of flood insurance makes the applicant ineligible for any financial assistance from SBA, including disaster assistance.

Executive Orders -- Floodplain Management and Wetland Protection (42 F.R. 26951 and 42 F.R. 26961) -- SBA discourages settlement in or development of a floodplain or a wetland. This statement is to notify all SBA loan applicants that such actions are hazardous to both life and property and should be avoided. The additional cost of flood preventive construction must be considered in addition to the possible loss of all assets and investments due to a future flood.

Occupational Safety and Health Act (15 U.S.C. 651 et seq.) -- This legislation authorizes the Occupational Safety and Health Administration in the Department of Labor to require businesses to modify facilities and procedures to protect employees or pay penalty fees. Businesses can be forced to cease operations or be prevented from starting operations in a new facility. Therefore, SBA may require additional information from an applicant to determine whether the business will be in compliance with OSHA regulations and allowed to operate its facility after the loan is approved and disbursed. Signing this form as an applicant is certification that the OSHA requirements that apply to the applicant business have been determined and that the applicant, to the best of its knowledge, is in compliance. Furthermore, applicant certifies that it will remain in compliance during the life of the loan.

Civil Rights Legislation -- All businesses receiving SBA financial assistance must agree not to discriminate in any business practice, including employment practices and services to the public on the basis of categories cited in 13 C.F.R., Parts 112, 113, and 117 of SBA Regulations. This includes making their goods and services available to handicapped clients or customers. All business borrowers will be required to display the "Equal Employment Opportunity Poster" prescribed by SBA.

Equal Credit Opportunity Act (15 U.S.C. 1691) -- The Federal Equal Credit Opportunity Act prohibits creditors from discriminating against credit applicants on the basis of race, color, religion, national origin, sex, marital status or age (provided the applicant has the capacity to enter into a binding contract); because all or part of the applicant's income derives from any public assistance program, or because the applicant has in good faith exercised any right under the Consumer Credit Protection Act.

Executive Order 11738 -- Environmental Protection (38 F.R. 251621) -- The Executive Order charges SBA with administering its loan programs in a manner that will result in effective enforcement of the Clean Air Act, the Federal Water Pollution Act and other environment protection legislation.

Debt Collection Act of 1982, Deficit Reduction Act of 1984 (31 U.S.C. 3701 et seq. and other titles) -- These laws require SBA to collect aggressively any loan payments which become delinquent. SBA must obtain your taxpayer identification number when you apply for a loan. If you receive a loan, and do not make payments as they come due, SBA may take one or more of the following actions: (1) report the status of your loan(s) to credit bureaus, (2) hire a collection agency to collect your loan, (3) offset your income tax refund or other amounts due to you from the Federal Government, (4) suspend or debar you or your company from doing business with the Federal Government, (5) refer your loan to the Department of Justice or other attorneys for litigation, or (6) foreclose on collateral or take other action permitted in the loan instruments.

Immigration Reform and Control Act of 1986 (Pub. L. 99-603) -- If you are an alien who was in this country illegally since before January 1, 1982, you may have been granted lawful temporary resident status by the United States Immigration and Naturalization Service pursuant to the Immigration Reform and Control Act of 1986. For five years from the date you are granted such status, you are not eligible for financial assistance from the SBA in the form of a loan guaranty under Section 7(a) of the Small Business Act unless you are disabled or a Cuban or Haitian entrant. When you sign this document, you are making the certification that the Immigration Reform and Control Act of 1986 does not apply to you, or if it does apply, more than five years have elapsed since you have been granted lawful temporary resident status pursuant to such 1986 legislation.

Lead-Based Paint Poisoning Prevention Act (42 U.S.C. 4821 et seq.)
Borrowers using SBA funds for the construction or rehabilitation of a residential structure are prohibited from using lead-based paint (as defined in SBA regulations) on all interior surfaces, whether accessible or not, and exterior surfaces, such as stairs, decks, porches, railings, windows and doors, which are readily accessible to children under 7 years of age. A "residential structure" is any home, apartment, hotel, motel, orphanage, boarding school, dormitory, day care center, extended care facility, college or other school housing, hospital, group practice or community facility and all other residential or institutional structures where persons reside.

Executive Order 12549, Debarment and Suspension 2 CFR 2700
1. The borrower or contractor certifies, by submission of its application for an SBA loan or bond guarantee, that neither it nor its principals are presently debarred, suspended, proposed for debarment, declared ineligible, or voluntarily excluded from participation in this transaction by any Federal department or agency.
2. Where the prospective lower tier participant is unable to certify to any of the statements in this certification, such prospective participants shall attach an explanation to the application.

Form 912 (1/2)

OMB APPROVAL NO.3245-0178
Expiration Date: 05/31/2019

United States of America

SMALL BUSINESS ADMINISTRATION

STATEMENT OF PERSONAL HISTORY

Please Read Carefully and Fully Complete: SBA uses Form 912 as one part of its assessment of program eligibility. Please reference SBA Regulations and Standard Operating Procedures if you have any questions about who must submit this form and where to submit it. For further information, please call SBA's Answer Desk at 1-800-U-ASK-SBA (1-800-827-5722), or check SBA's website at www.sba.gov. **DO NOT SEND COMPLETED FORMS TO OMB as this will delay the processing of your application; send forms to the address provided by your lender or SBA representative.**

1a. Name and Address of Applicant (Firm Name)(Street, City, State, ZIP Code and E-mail)

SBA District/Disaster Area Office

Amount Applied for (when applicable) | File No. (if known)

1b. Personal Statement of: (State name in full, if no middle name, state (NMN), or if initial only, indicate initial.) List all former names used, and dates each name was used. Use separate sheet if necessary.

First   Middle   Last

2. Give the percentage of ownership in the small business | Social Security No.

3. Date of Birth (Month, day, and year)

4. Place of Birth: (City & State or Foreign Country)

If applicable, Name and Address of participating lender or surety co.

5. U.S. Citizen? ☐ YES ☐ NO **INITIALS:**
If no, are you a Lawful Permanent resident alien? ☐ YES ☐ NO Alien Registration number
If no, country of citzenship:

6. Present residence address:
From:
To:
Address:

Most recent prior address (omit if over 10 years ago):
From:
To:
Address:

Home Telephone No. (Include Area Code):
Business Telephone No. (Include Area Code):

PLEASE SEE REVERSE SIDE FOR EXPLANATION REGARDING DISCLOSURE OF INFORMATION AND THE USES OF SUCH INFORMATION.

YOU MUST INITIAL YOUR RESPONSES TO QUESTIONS 5,7,8 AND 9.

IF YOU ANSWER "YES" TO 7, 8, OR 9, YOU MUST FURNISH DETAILS ON A SEPARATE SHEET. INCLUDE DATES, LOCATION, FINES, SENTENCES, MISDEMEANOR OR FELONY, DATES OF PAROLE/PROBATION, UNPAID FINES OR PENALTIES, NAME(S) UNDER WHICH CHARGED, AND ANY OTHER PERTINENT INFORMATION. AN ARREST OR CONVICTION RECORD WILL NOT NECESSARILY DISQUALIFY YOU; HOWEVER, AN UNTRUTHFUL ANSWER WILL CAUSE YOUR APPLICATION TO BE DENIED AND SUBJECT YOU TO OTHER PENALTIES AS NOTED BELOW.

7. Are you presently subject to an indictment, criminal information, arraignment, or other means by which formal criminal charges are brought in any jurisdiction?
☐ Yes ☐ No **INITIALS:**

8. Have you been arrested in the past six months for any criminal offense?
☐ Yes ☐ No **INITIALS:**

9. For any criminal offense – other than a minor vehicle violation – have you ever:1) been convicted; 2) pleaded guilty; 3) pleaded nolo contendere; 4) been placed on pretrial diversion; or 5) been placed on any form of parole or probation (including probation before judgment).
☐ Yes ☐ No **INITIALS:**

10. I authorize the Small Business Administration to request criminal record information about me from criminal justice agencies for the purpose of determining my eligibility for programs authorized by the Small Business Act and the Small Business Investment Act.

CAUTION - PENALTIES FOR FALSE STATEMENTS: Knowingly making a false statement on this form is a violation of Federal law and could result in criminal prosecution, significant civil penalties, and a denial of your loan, surety bond, or other program participation. A false statement is punishable under 18 USC 1001 and 3571 by imprisonment of not more than five years and/or a fine of up to $250,000; under 15 USC 645 by imprisonment of not more than two years and/or a fine of not more than $5,000; and, if submitted to a Federally insured institution, under 18 USC 1014 by imprisonment of not more than thirty years and/or a fine of not more than $1,000,000.

Signature | Title | Date

Agency Use Only

11. ☐ Fingerprints Waived   Date   Approving Authority

☐ Fingerprints Required   Date   Approving Authority

Date Sent to OPS

12. ☐ Cleared for Processing   Date   Approving Authority

13. ☐ Request a Character Evaluation   Date   Approving Authority

(Required whenever 7, 8 or 9 are answered "yes" even if cleared for processing.)

SBA 912 (4-2016) SOP 5010 Previous Edition Obsolete

Form 912 (2/2)
NOTICES REQUIRED BY LAW

The following is a brief summary of the laws applicable to this solicitation of information.

PLEASE NOTE: The estimated burden for completing this form is 15 minutes per response. You are not required to respond to any collection of information unless it displays a currently valid OMB approval number. If you wish to submit comments on the burden for completing this form,.direct these comments to U.S. Small Business Administration, Chief, AIB, 409 3rd St., S.W., Washington D.C. 20416 and Desk Officer for the Small Business Administration, Office of Management and Budget, New Executive Office Building, Room 10202, Washington, D.C. 20503. OMB Approval 3245-0178

Paperwork Reduction Act (44 U.S.C. Chapter 35)

SBA is collecting the information on this form to make a character and credit eligibility decision to fund or deny you a loan or other form of assistance. The information is required in order for SBA to have sufficient information to determine whether to provide you with the requested assistance. The information collected may be checked against criminal history indices of the Federal Bureau of Investigation.

Privacy Act (5 U.S.C. § 552a)

Any person can request to see or get copies of any personal information that SBA has in his or her file, when that file is retrieved by individual identifiers, such as name or social security numbers. Requests for information about another party may be denied unless SBA has the written permission of the individual to release the information to the requestor or unless the information is subject to disclosure under the Freedom of Information Act.

Under the provisions of the Privacy Act, you are not required to provide your social security number. Failure to provide your social security number may not affect any right, benefit or privilege to which you are entitled. Disclosures of name and other personal identifiers are, however, required for a benefit, as SBA requires an individual seeking assistance from SBA to provide it with sufficient information for it to make a character determination. In determining whether an individual is of good character, SBA considers the person's integrity, candor, and disposition toward criminal actions. In making loans pursuant to section 7(a)(6) the Small Business Act (the Act), 15 USC § 636 (a)(6), SBA is required to have reasonable assurance that the loan is of sound value and will be repaid or that it is in the best interest of the Government to grant the assistance requested. Additionally, SBA is specifically authorized to verify your criminal history, or lack thereof, pursuant to section 7(a)(1)(B), 15 USC § 636(a)(1)(B). Further, for all forms of assistance, SBA is authorized to make all investigations necessary to ensure that a person has not engaged in acts that violate or will violate the Act or the Small Business Investment Act,15 USC §§ 634(b)(11) and 687b(a). For these purposes, you are asked to voluntarily provide your social security number to assist SBA in making a character determination and to distinguish you from other individuals with the same or similar name or other personal identifier.

When the information collected on this form indicates a violation or potential violation of law, whether civil, criminal, or administrative in nature, SBA may refer it to the appropriate agency, whether Federal, State, local, or foreign, charged with responsibility for or otherwise involved in investigation, prosecution, enforcement or prevention of such violations. See 74 Fed. Reg. 14890 (2009) for other published routine uses.

Form G-845 (1/3)

Verification Request

Department of Homeland Security
U.S. Citizenship and Immigration Services

**USCIS
Form G-845**
OMB No. 1615-0101
Expires: 05/31/2018

▶ **START HERE - Type or print in black ink.**

Part 1. Information From the Registered Agency

NOTE: Only the Registered Agency should complete this information.

To: U.S. Citizenship and Immigration Services (USCIS)

Attn: USCIS SAVE Program Status Verification Office

_____

_____

_____

Stamp, type, or print the name, address, and ZIP Code of the Registered Agency. (**Print clearly since USCIS may use agency address below with a No. 10 window envelope.**)

From:

_____

_____

_____

_____

Applicant Information

Immigration Document Number

1.a. Alien Registration Number (A-Number)

A- ▶ [   ]

1.b. Form I-94 Number (Arrival-Departure Record)

▶ [   ]

1.c. Other Immigration Number

[   ]

1.d. Name or Form Number of Document Containing the Other Immigration Number

[   ]

Applicant's Full Name as Shown on the Immigration Document

2.a. Last Name [   ]

2.b. First Name [   ]

2.c. Middle Name [   ]

3. Case Verification Number

[   ]

4. Date of Birth   (mm/dd/yyyy) [   ]

5. Social Security Number

▶ [   ]

6. Student and Exchange Visitor Information System (SEVIS) Number

[   ]

7. Citizenship or Nationality

[   ]

Documents Attached (Select all that apply)

8.a. ☐ Photocopy of most recently issued immigration document attached. Ensure copies are legible and made from an original document. If the immigration document is printed on both sides, attach a copy of the front **and** back.

8.b. ☐ Other Information Attached (Specify Documents)

[   ]

Benefits Sought

9.a. ☐ Background Check

9.b. ☐ Driver's License/ID

9.c. ☐ Education Grant/Loan/Work Study

9.d. ☐ Employment Authorization

9.e. ☐ Food Stamps

9.f. ☐ Housing Assistance

9.g. ☐ Medicaid/Medical Assistance

9.h. ☐ Social Security Number

9.i. ☐ SSI or RSDI

9.j. ☐ TANF

9.k. ☐ Unemployment Insurance

9.l. ☐ Other (Specify)

[   ]

Form G-845 (2/3

Applicant's Last Name	Applicant's First Name	Case Verification Number

Part 1. Information From the Registered Agency (continued)

Registered Agency Information

10. Registered Agency Case Number

Full Name of Agency Official

11.a. Last Name

11.b. First Name

12. Title of Agency Official

13.a. Daytime Telephone Number (Include Area Code)

13.b. Extension Number (if applicable)

14. Fax Number (if any) (Include Area Code)

15. Date Request Completed
(mm/dd/yyyy)

16. Registered Agency Comments (if any)

Part 2. USCIS Responses

NOTE: Only USCIS should complete this information.

Upon review of these documents, information submitted, and our records, we find the following for the applicant:

1. ☐ **Lawful Permanent Resident** of the United States

2. ☐ **Conditional Permanent Resident** of the United States

3. ☐ Applicant is **employment authorized** in the United States as indicated:

☐ No Expiration Date (Indefinite)

☐ Expiration Date
(mm/dd/yyyy)

☐ Previous Employment Authorization Dates

Start Date (mm/dd/yyyy) End Date (mm/dd/yyyy)

4. ☐ Applicant is **not employment authorized** in the United States

5. ☐ Applicant has an **application pending** for the following USCIS benefit:

6. ☐ Applicant was **granted asylum or refugee** status in the United States

7. ☐ Applicant was **paroled** into the United States under section 212 of the Immigration and Nationality Act (INA).

☐ No Expiration Date (Indefinite)

☐ Parole Granted Date
(mm/dd/yyyy)

☐ Parole Expiration Date
(mm/dd/yyyy)

8. ☐ **Conditional entrant of the United States**

9. ☐ **Nonimmigrant** (Specify type or class and expiration date)

Type or Class

Expiration Date (mm/dd/yyyy)

10. ☐ **U.S. Citizen**

Form G-845 (3/3)

Applicant's Last Name	Applicant's First Name	Case Verification Number

Part 2. USCIS Responses (continued)

11. ☐ **Cuban/Haitian entrant** of the United States

12. ☐ **American Indian** born in Canada to whom the provisions of INA 289 apply.

Date Status Recognized
(mm/dd/yyyy) _____

13. ☐ **Mexican Born Member** of the Texas or Oklahoma Band of **Kickapoo Indians**

   a. ☐ I-872 Issuance Date:
      (mm/dd/yyyy) _____

      COA (KIC or KIP)
      _____

   b. ☐ Other foreign born American Indian Date of Entry:
      (mm/dd/yyyy) _____

      COA
      _____

14. ☐ **Deferred Action for Childhood Arrivals** (DACA)

15. ☐ **Temporary Protected Status** (TPS)

16. ☐ **Deferred Action Status**

17. ☐ **VAWA Self-Petitioner**

   a. ☐ Pending prima facie VAWA self-petition

   b. ☐ Approved VAWA self-petition

18. ☐ **Withholding of Removal**

19. ☐ USCIS is searching indices for further information

20. ☐ This document is **not valid** because it appears to be: (Select all that apply)

   a. ☐ Expired

   b. ☐ Altered

   c. ☐ Counterfeit

Part 3. USCIS Comments

NOTE: Only USCIS should complete this information.

1. ☐ Unable to process request without an original consent of disclosure statement signed by the applicant. Resubmit request.

2. ☐ No determination can be made because insufficient information was submitted. Obtain a copy of the applicant's most recently issued immigration document. Submit a new request.

3. ☐ No determination can be made without seeing both sides of the applicant's immigration document. Attach copies (front and back) of the applicant's most recently issued immigration document and submit a new request.

4. ☐ Copy provided of applicant's immigration document is illegible. Submit a new request with legible documents.

5. ☐ Unable to verify status based on the document provided. If this is the applicant's most recently issued immigration document, refer the applicant to the document issuing authority.

6. ☐ Other

_____
_____
_____
_____
_____
_____
_____
_____
_____
_____
_____
_____

USCIS Stamp

Franchise Form 2462 (instructions)

INSTRUCTIONS FOR USE OF SBA FORM 2462
ADDENDUM TO FRANCHISE AGREEMENT

SBA has issued a revised version of the Addendum to Franchise Agreement (SBA Form 2462) which became effective February 14, 2017. SBA Policy Notice 5000-1941 explains updates made to the franchise review process for the 7(a) and 504 loan programs.

SBA Form 2462 has **three** locations with drop down menu options at the beginning of the form (see example below). Once a drop down option is chosen (i.e. #1 "Franchise" #2 "Franchisor" and #3 "Franchisee"), the user must hit "tab" key to automatically populate the appropriate term in all fields.

Example of Drop-Down Options

Once the drop down options have populated in all three locations, the remaining fillable fields must be completed manually (see example below). These fields will either be blank or contain the language "(Enter type of)" or "(type of agreement)." When completing SBA Form 2462, the text may not be altered except to insert the information required to complete the form.

Example of Fillable Fields to be Completed Manually

FORCED SALE OF ASSETS

- If Franchisor _____ has the option to purchase the business personal assets upon default or termination of the Franchise _____ Agreement and the parties are unable to agree on the value of the assets, the value will be determined by an appraiser chosen by both parties. If the Franchisee _____ owns the real estate where the franchisee _____ location is operating, Franchisee _____ will not be required to sell the real estate upon default or termination, but Franchisee _____ may be required to lease the real estate for the remainder of the (enter type of) _____ term (excluding additional renewals) for fair market value.

Note to Parties: This Addendum only addresses "affiliation" between the Franchisor _____ and Franchisee _____. Additionally, the applicant Franchisee _____ and the (type of agreement) _____ system must meet all SBA eligibility requirements.

Franchise Form 2462 (1/2)

ADDENDUM TO <u>Franchise</u> _____[1] **AGREEMENT**

THIS ADDENDUM ("Addendum") is made and entered into on _____, 20____, by and

between _____ ("**Franchisor** "),

located at _____, and

_____ ("**Franchisee** "),

located at _____.

<u>Franchisor</u> and <u>Franchisee</u> entered into a <u>Franchise</u> Agreement on _____, 20___, (such Agreement, together with any amendments, the "<u>Franchise</u> Agreement"). <u>Franchisee</u> is applying for financing(s) from a lender in which funding is provided with the assistance of the U. S. Small Business Administration ("SBA"). SBA requires the execution of this Addendum as a condition for obtaining SBA-assisted financing.

In consideration of the mutual promises below and for good and valuable consideration, the receipt and sufficiency of which the parties acknowledge the parties agree that notwithstanding any other terms in the <u>Franchise</u> Agreement:

CHANGE OF OWNERSHIP

- If <u>Franchisee</u> is proposing to transfer a partial interest in <u>Franchisee</u> and <u>Franchisor</u> has an option to purchase or a right of first refusal with respect to that partial interest, <u>Franchisor</u> may exercise such option or right only if the proposed transferee is not a current owner or family member of a current owner of <u>Franchisee</u>. If the <u>Franchisor</u> 's consent is required for any transfer (full or partial), <u>Franchisor</u> will not unreasonably withhold such consent. In the event of an approved transfer of the <u>(Enter type of)</u> interest or any portion thereof, the transferor will not be liable for the actions of the transferee <u>Franchisee</u>.

FORCED SALE OF ASSETS

- If <u>Franchisor</u> has the option to purchase the business personal assets upon default or termination of the <u>Franchise</u> Agreement and the parties are unable to agree on the value of the assets, the value will be determined by an appraiser chosen by both parties. If the <u>Franchisee</u> owns the real estate where the <u>franchisee</u> location is operating, <u>Franchisee</u> will not be required to sell the real estate upon default or termination, but <u>Franchisee</u> may be required to lease the real estate for the remainder of the <u>(enter type of)</u> term (excluding additional renewals) for fair market value.

---

[1] While relationships established under license, jobber, dealer and similar agreements are not generally described as "franchise" relationships, if such relationships meet the Federal Trade Commission's (FTC's) definition of a franchise (see 16 CFR § 436), they are treated by SBA as franchise relationships for franchise affiliation determinations per 13 CFR § 121.301(f)(5).

112

Franchise Form 2462 (2/2)

COVENANTS

- If the _Franchisee_ owns the real estate where the _franchisee_ location is operating, _Franchisor_ has not and will not during the term of the _Franchise_ Agreement record against the real estate any restrictions on the use of the property, including any restrictive covenants, branding covenants or environmental use restrictions. If any such restrictions are currently recorded against the _Franchisee_ 's real estate, they must be removed in order for the _Franchisee_ to obtain SBA-assisted financing.

EMPLOYMENT

- _Franchisor_ will not directly control (hire, fire or schedule) _Franchisee_ 's employees. For temporary personnel franchises, the temporary employees will be employed by the _Franchisee_ not the _Franchisor_ .

As to the referenced _Franchise_ Agreement, this Addendum automatically terminates when SBA no longer has any interest in any SBA-assisted financing provided to the _Franchisee_ .

Except as amended by this Addendum, the _Franchise_ Agreement remains in full force and effect according to its terms.

Franchisor and _Franchisee_ acknowledge that submission of false information to SBA, or the withholding of material information from SBA, can result in criminal prosecution under 18 U.S.C. 1001 and other provisions, including liability for treble damages under the False Claims Act, 31 U.S.C. §§ 3729 - 3733.

Authorized Representative of FRANCHISOR :

By: _____

Print Name: _____

Title: _____

Authorized Representative of FRANCHISEE :

By: _____

Print Name: _____

Title: _____

Note to Parties: This Addendum only addresses "affiliation" between the _Franchisor_ and _Franchisee_ . Additionally, the applicant _Franchisee_ and the _(type of agreement)_ system must meet all SBA eligibility requirements.

SBA Form 2462 (02-17)   Page 2

Insurance Business Personal Property (for content)

ACORD®	**EVIDENCE OF PROPERTY INSURANCE**	DATE (MM/DD/YYYY)

THIS EVIDENCE OF PROPERTY INSURANCE IS ISSUED AS A MATTER OF INFORMATION ONLY AND CONFERS NO RIGHTS UPON THE ADDITIONAL INTEREST NAMED BELOW. THIS EVIDENCE DOES NOT AFFIRMATIVELY OR NEGATIVELY AMEND, EXTEND OR ALTER THE COVERAGE AFFORDED BY THE POLICIES BELOW. THIS EVIDENCE OF INSURANCE DOES NOT CONSTITUTE A CONTRACT BETWEEN THE ISSUING INSURER(S), AUTHORIZED REPRESENTATIVE OR PRODUCER, AND THE ADDITIONAL INTEREST.

AGENCY	PHONE (A/C, No, Ext):	COMPANY
FAX (A/C, No):	E-MAIL ADDRESS:	
CODE:	SUB CODE:	
AGENCY CUSTOMER ID #:		
INSURED		LOAN NUMBER	POLICY NUMBER
		EFFECTIVE DATE	EXPIRATION DATE	CONTINUED UNTIL TERMINATED IF CHECKED
		THIS REPLACES PRIOR EVIDENCE DATED:

PROPERTY INFORMATION

LOCATION/DESCRIPTION

THE POLICIES OF INSURANCE LISTED BELOW HAVE BEEN ISSUED TO THE INSURED NAMED ABOVE FOR THE POLICY PERIOD INDICATED. NOTWITHSTANDING ANY REQUIREMENT, TERM OR CONDITION OF ANY CONTRACT OR OTHER DOCUMENT WITH RESPECT TO WHICH THIS EVIDENCE OF PROPERTY INSURANCE MAY BE ISSUED OR MAY PERTAIN, THE INSURANCE AFFORDED BY THE POLICIES DESCRIBED HEREIN IS SUBJECT TO ALL THE TERMS, EXCLUSIONS AND CONDITIONS OF SUCH POLICIES. LIMITS SHOWN MAY HAVE BEEN REDUCED BY PAID CLAIMS.

COVERAGE INFORMATION   PERILS INSURED | BASIC | BROAD | SPECIAL

COVERAGE / PERILS / FORMS	AMOUNT OF INSURANCE	DEDUCTIBLE

REMARKS (Including Special Conditions)

CANCELLATION

SHOULD ANY OF THE ABOVE DESCRIBED POLICIES BE CANCELLED BEFORE THE EXPIRATION DATE THEREOF, NOTICE WILL BE DELIVERED IN ACCORDANCE WITH THE POLICY PROVISIONS.

ADDITIONAL INTEREST

NAME AND ADDRESS	ADDITIONAL INSURED	LENDER'S LOSS PAYABLE	LOSS PAYEE
	MORTGAGEE		
	LOAN #		
	AUTHORIZED REPRESENTATIVE		

ACORD 27 (2016/03)

Insurance Business Personal Property (for Building and/or content)

ACORD® **EVIDENCE OF COMMERCIAL PROPERTY INSURANCE**

DATE (MM/DD/YYYY)

THIS EVIDENCE OF COMMERCIAL PROPERTY INSURANCE IS ISSUED AS A MATTER OF INFORMATION ONLY AND CONFERS NO RIGHTS UPON THE ADDITIONAL INTEREST NAMED BELOW. THIS EVIDENCE DOES NOT AFFIRMATIVELY OR NEGATIVELY AMEND, EXTEND OR ALTER THE COVERAGE AFFORDED BY THE POLICIES BELOW. THIS EVIDENCE OF INSURANCE DOES NOT CONSTITUTE A CONTRACT BETWEEN THE ISSUING INSURER(S), AUTHORIZED REPRESENTATIVE OR PRODUCER, AND THE ADDITIONAL INTEREST.

PRODUCER NAME, CONTACT PERSON AND ADDRESS	PHONE (A/C, No. Ext):	COMPANY NAME AND ADDRESS	NAIC NO:

FAX (A/C, No):	E-MAIL ADDRESS:	IF MULTIPLE COMPANIES, COMPLETE SEPARATE FORM FOR EACH

CODE:	SUB CODE:	POLICY TYPE

AGENCY CUSTOMER ID #:

NAMED INSURED AND ADDRESS	LOAN NUMBER	POLICY NUMBER

	EFFECTIVE DATE	EXPIRATION DATE	CONTINUED UNTIL TERMINATED IF CHECKED

ADDITIONAL NAMED INSURED(S)	THIS REPLACES PRIOR EVIDENCE DATED:

PROPERTY INFORMATION (ACORD 101 may be attached if more space is required) ☐ BUILDING OR ☐ BUSINESS PERSONAL PROPERTY

LOCATION / DESCRIPTION

THE POLICIES OF INSURANCE LISTED BELOW HAVE BEEN ISSUED TO THE INSURED NAMED ABOVE FOR THE POLICY PERIOD INDICATED. NOTWITHSTANDING ANY REQUIREMENT, TERM OR CONDITION OF ANY CONTRACT OR OTHER DOCUMENT WITH RESPECT TO WHICH THIS EVIDENCE OF PROPERTY INSURANCE MAY BE ISSUED OR MAY PERTAIN, THE INSURANCE AFFORDED BY THE POLICIES DESCRIBED HEREIN IS SUBJECT TO ALL THE TERMS, EXCLUSIONS AND CONDITIONS OF SUCH POLICIES. LIMITS SHOWN MAY HAVE BEEN REDUCED BY PAID CLAIMS.

COVERAGE INFORMATION PERILS INSURED | BASIC | BROAD | SPECIAL |

COMMERCIAL PROPERTY COVERAGE AMOUNT OF INSURANCE: $				DED:

	YES	NO	N/A	
☐ BUSINESS INCOME ☐ RENTAL VALUE				If YES, LIMIT:	Actual Loss Sustained; # of months:
BLANKET COVERAGE				If YES, indicate value(s) reported on property identified above: $
TERRORISM COVERAGE				Attach Disclosure Notice / DEC
IS THERE A TERRORISM-SPECIFIC EXCLUSION?				
IS DOMESTIC TERRORISM EXCLUDED?				
LIMITED FUNGUS COVERAGE				If YES, LIMIT:	DED:
FUNGUS EXCLUSION (If "YES", specify organization's form used)				
REPLACEMENT COST				
AGREED VALUE				
COINSURANCE				If YES, %
EQUIPMENT BREAKDOWN (If Applicable)				If YES, LIMIT:	DED:
ORDINANCE OR LAW - Coverage for loss to undamaged portion of bldg				If YES, LIMIT:	DED:
- Demolition Costs				If YES, LIMIT:	DED:
- Incr. Cost of Construction				If YES, LIMIT:	DED:
EARTH MOVEMENT (If Applicable)				If YES, LIMIT:	DED:
FLOOD (If Applicable)				If YES, LIMIT:	DED:
WIND / HAIL INCL ☐ YES ☐ NO Subject to Different Provisions:				If YES, LIMIT:	DED:
NAMED STORM INCL ☐ YES ☐ NO Subject to Different Provisions:				If YES, LIMIT:	DED:
PERMISSION TO WAIVE SUBROGATION IN FAVOR OF MORTGAGE HOLDER PRIOR TO LOSS				

CANCELLATION

SHOULD ANY OF THE ABOVE DESCRIBED POLICIES BE CANCELLED BEFORE THE EXPIRATION DATE THEREOF, NOTICE WILL BE DELIVERED IN ACCORDANCE WITH THE POLICY PROVISIONS.

ADDITIONAL INTEREST

☐ CONTRACT OF SALE ☐ MORTGAGEE	☐ LENDER'S LOSS PAYABLE	☐ LOSS PAYEE	LENDER SERVICING AGENT NAME AND ADDRESS

NAME AND ADDRESS	
	AUTHORIZED REPRESENTATIVE

ACORD 28 (2016/03) The ACORD name and logo are registered marks of ACORD

Insurance General Liability

ACORD® | **CERTIFICATE OF LIABILITY INSURANCE** | DATE (MM/DD/YYYY)

THIS CERTIFICATE IS ISSUED AS A MATTER OF INFORMATION ONLY AND CONFERS NO RIGHTS UPON THE CERTIFICATE HOLDER. THIS CERTIFICATE DOES NOT AFFIRMATIVELY OR NEGATIVELY AMEND, EXTEND OR ALTER THE COVERAGE AFFORDED BY THE POLICIES BELOW. THIS CERTIFICATE OF INSURANCE DOES NOT CONSTITUTE A CONTRACT BETWEEN THE ISSUING INSURER(S), AUTHORIZED REPRESENTATIVE OR PRODUCER, AND THE CERTIFICATE HOLDER.

IMPORTANT: If the certificate holder is an ADDITIONAL INSURED, the policy(ies) must have ADDITIONAL INSURED provisions or be endorsed. If SUBROGATION IS WAIVED, subject to the terms and conditions of the policy, certain policies may require an endorsement. A statement on this certificate does not confer rights to the certificate holder in lieu of such endorsement(s).

PRODUCER	CONTACT NAME:		
	PHONE (A/C, No, Ext):		FAX (A/C, No):
	E-MAIL ADDRESS:		
	INSURER(S) AFFORDING COVERAGE		NAIC #
	INSURER A :		
INSURED	INSURER B :		
	INSURER C :		
	INSURER D :		
	INSURER E :		
	INSURER F :		

COVERAGES CERTIFICATE NUMBER: REVISION NUMBER:

THIS IS TO CERTIFY THAT THE POLICIES OF INSURANCE LISTED BELOW HAVE BEEN ISSUED TO THE INSURED NAMED ABOVE FOR THE POLICY PERIOD INDICATED. NOTWITHSTANDING ANY REQUIREMENT, TERM OR CONDITION OF ANY CONTRACT OR OTHER DOCUMENT WITH RESPECT TO WHICH THIS CERTIFICATE MAY BE ISSUED OR MAY PERTAIN, THE INSURANCE AFFORDED BY THE POLICIES DESCRIBED HEREIN IS SUBJECT TO ALL THE TERMS, EXCLUSIONS AND CONDITIONS OF SUCH POLICIES. LIMITS SHOWN MAY HAVE BEEN REDUCED BY PAID CLAIMS.

INSR LTR	TYPE OF INSURANCE	ADDL INSD	SUBR WVD	POLICY NUMBER	POLICY EFF (MM/DD/YYYY)	POLICY EXP (MM/DD/YYYY)	LIMITS	
	COMMERCIAL GENERAL LIABILITY						EACH OCCURRENCE	$
	☐ CLAIMS-MADE ☐ OCCUR						DAMAGE TO RENTED PREMISES (Ea occurrence)	$
							MED EXP (Any one person)	$
							PERSONAL & ADV INJURY	$
	GEN'L AGGREGATE LIMIT APPLIES PER:						GENERAL AGGREGATE	$
	☐ POLICY ☐ PRO-JECT ☐ LOC						PRODUCTS - COMP/OP AGG	$
	OTHER:							$
	AUTOMOBILE LIABILITY						COMBINED SINGLE LIMIT (Ea accident)	$
	☐ ANY AUTO						BODILY INJURY (Per person)	$
	☐ OWNED AUTOS ONLY ☐ SCHEDULED AUTOS						BODILY INJURY (Per accident)	$
	☐ HIRED AUTOS ONLY ☐ NON-OWNED AUTOS ONLY						PROPERTY DAMAGE (Per accident)	$
								$
	☐ UMBRELLA LIAB ☐ OCCUR						EACH OCCURRENCE	$
	☐ EXCESS LIAB ☐ CLAIMS-MADE						AGGREGATE	$
	☐ DED ☐ RETENTION $							$
	WORKERS COMPENSATION AND EMPLOYERS' LIABILITY Y / N						☐ PER STATUTE ☐ OTH-ER	
	ANY PROPRIETOR/PARTNER/EXECUTIVE OFFICER/MEMBER EXCLUDED? (Mandatory in NH)	N/A					E.L. EACH ACCIDENT	$
							E.L. DISEASE - EA EMPLOYEE	$
	If yes, describe under DESCRIPTION OF OPERATIONS below						E.L. DISEASE - POLICY LIMIT	$

DESCRIPTION OF OPERATIONS / LOCATIONS / VEHICLES (ACORD 101, Additional Remarks Schedule, may be attached if more space is required)

CERTIFICATE HOLDER	CANCELLATION
	SHOULD ANY OF THE ABOVE DESCRIBED POLICIES BE CANCELLED BEFORE THE EXPIRATION DATE THEREOF, NOTICE WILL BE DELIVERED IN ACCORDANCE WITH THE POLICY PROVISIONS.
	AUTHORIZED REPRESENTATIVE

ACORD 25 (2016/03) The ACORD name and logo are registered marks of ACORD

www.ingramcontent.com/pod-product-compliance
Lightning Source LLC
Chambersburg PA
CBHW081546220326
41598CB00036B/6582